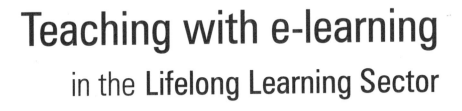

Teaching with e-learning

in the Lifelong Learning Sector

Second edition

Teaching with e-learning
in the Lifelong Learning Sector

Second edition

Chris Hill

LearningMatters

First published in 2003 as *Teaching Using Information and Learning Technology in Further Education*
Reprinted in 2006
Second edition published in 2008
Reprinted in 2008

British Library Cataloguing in Publication Data
A CIP record for this book is available from the British Library.

ISBN 978 1 84445 135 7

Cover design by Topics – The Creative Partnership
Text design by Code 5 Design Associates Ltd
Project management by Deer Park Productions, Tavistock, Devon
Typeset by Pantek Arts Ltd, Maidstone, Kent
Printed and bound in Great Britain by Bell & Bain Ltd, Glasgow

Learning Matters Ltd
33 Southernhay East
Exeter EX1 1NX
Tel: 01392 215560
info@learningmatters.co.uk
www.learningmatters.co.uk

Contents

Acknowledgements

The Professional Standards for teachers, tutors and trainees in the Learning and Skills Sector were published in 2007 by Lifelong Learning UK (throughout).

The 'eclipse' diagram (Chapter 2): Markos Tiris © LSN (reproduced by permission of Becta).

Thanks to Professor Phil Race for permission to use the 'ripples on a pond' model of learning (Chapter 3); Western Colleges Consortium for use of Virtual Campus screenshot (Chapter 5); City of Bath College for WebCT screenshot (Chapter 5).

The e-learning fan (Chapter 4): Jenny Scribbins/Bob Powell © Becta (diagram published on Ferl website: ferl.qia.org.uk).

The MLE diagram (Chapter 5): Bob Powell © Becta (diagram published on Ferl website: ferl.qia.org.uk).

Internet Explorer screenshot(s) (Chapter 5) reprinted by permission from Microsoft Corporation who own the trademark.

This book is dedicated to Kath for not asking too many questions about what I was doing in the study all that time, and to Richard and David for leaving home and giving me the space to write it.

1
Introduction

This chapter will help you to:

- **preview the content and format of this book;**
- **use the book productively;**
- **identify and explain key ideas behind the book.**

Learning has always been part of the human experience and where there is learning, more often than not there is teaching. Some of our ideas about teaching go back a long way, yet are still valid. In Greece in the fifth century BC, Socrates was teaching very effectively by the extensive use of questions and telling his learners very little at all. Yet our understanding of teaching and learning is still imperfect and the results unpredictable. What works well with one group of learners may not work with another group. Indeed, a teaching strategy that works well with a group one day may not work at all with the same learners the next day. Every learning occasion is unique.

All this means that anyone engaged in the art of teaching needs all the help they can possibly have. The information technology explosion since the second half of the twentieth century has provided many more tools to help the learning process. This book endeavours to enable teachers of adults to explore how they can exploit the potential of the new tools.

However, this is not a book about information technology. It is a book about teaching and learning. Information technology is presented not as an end in itself, but as a tool in the toolkit that resourceful teachers can draw on. As a reader of this book, whether or not you are a practising teacher or trainer, you are already an expert at learning. Just look at some of the things that you have learned – to communicate, to build relationships, to find your way around. You may be more or less aware of that learning process. This book is about adding the potential of information technology to what you know and can do already. The use of information technology for the purpose of teaching and learning is called information and learning technology (ILT) and E-learning is the key element of ILT.

Who is this book for?

This book is written for those working in, or intending to work in, the Learning and Skills sector. In England and Wales, further education was initially defined in the 1944 Education Act. In the 1988 Education Act it was defined as:

(a) full and part time education and training for persons over compulsory school age (including vocational, social, physical and recreational training); and (b) organised leisure-time occupation provided in connection with the provision of such education.

All this really tells you is that further education is to do with adults learning. Adults undertake organised learning in many different settings and the ideas in this book are relevant to them all, although I will focus on the formal Learning and Skills sector. This sector is named after the organisation responsible for funding it in England – the Learning and Skills Council. It includes not only the 400 or so FE and Sixth Form colleges, but also specialist colleges, adult and community learning (ACL), work-based learning (WBL) and offender learning. Although the names and funding set-ups may be different, there are equivalents in Wales, Northern Ireland and Scotland. Confusingly, I have noticed that politicians are increasingly using the term 'further education' to cover the whole Learning and Skills sector and the 2006 White Paper, *Further Education Reform: Raising Skills, Improving Life Chances*, refers to 'colleges and training providers'.

This broad coverage is why I refer to learners more often than students. A nurse teaching colleagues in order to update skills has learners, not students. It is also why I refer to learning providers rather than colleges, Adult Education Centres, Training Centres and so on. I know that 'learning provider' is not a term that comes up in everyday conversation, but it does cover everyone. And whilst we are setting out some basics, I usually refer to teachers or tutors, but include in the term trainers, lecturers, facilitators, mentors, instructors and any other title you care to think of.

The book is written both for existing teachers seeking to broaden their range of teaching strategies and for teachers in training who want to develop understanding and skills as the basis of a successful and effective career. ILT is so new that all of us are learning about it.

Because the main focus of the book is learning and not technology, there is no need to be too frustrated by the fact that you do not have access to every bit of kit mentioned. However, there is no harm in dreaming what you could do with powerful, portable multimedia computers with all the peripherals you can imagine – scanner, colour laser printer, digital camcorder, digital camera, plotter, internet-enabled mobile phone with built-in camera, video-conference suite, etc. In reality, most of us have a limited range of facilities although over time you would expect better technology to become more accessible. You should find out what is available and use it effectively. You are limited more by your imagination than the lack of kit.

I want to tell you a little about myself in order to set what I write in context. I am manager of the East Midlands Regional Support Centre (RSC), based at Loughborough College. This is one of thirteen RSCs funded mainly by the LSC and the funding councils of Wales, Northern Ireland and Scotland. It's the job of each RSC to support and stimulate innovation in learning in its region. Note that it says innovation in learning, not innovation in e-learning. That is significant and a theme that recurs throughout this book. Find out where your local RSC is and make contact. Ask to join its mailing lists.

Before that, I worked as a teacher in a medium-sized Further Education college in the English West Country with a specific responsibility for developing the use of ILT. I have been involved with the educational use of IT since the late 1970s when my colleague chose to spend several days typing all the questions from our stock of past A level economics exam papers into a word processor which then lost them. I set up geography fieldwork exercises on Commodore PET machines with 8k of memory (less than half the size of an empty Word document) and experienced the excitement of a room of twelve BBC computers all linked together. At each stage we used the computer equipment as a more or less effective tool to enable learners to learn. By the time I left, in 2003, the college had an excellent computer network and a good range of IT kit. Most significantly, the emphasis had noticeably shifted from the technology to learning, but there was still a long way to go.

Unfamiliar language, initialisms and acronyms

In any new area of study you have to learn a new language. Until you are familiar with it, the new language can make you feel excluded, although it does give greater precision once you develop your understanding. I have tried to avoid too many assumptions with regard to the terms I use, but some are bound to have crept through. If that happens, you should seek to clarify the meaning, either by asking colleagues or by using reference sources such as Whatis or Webopedia on the internet, and then learn to use them appropriately. To help with acronyms and initialisms (my wife, who teaches English language, tells me that there is difference), I have provided a list of the most common at the end of the book.

Features of the book and how to use them

Chapter 3 sets out some principles of learning and I have applied them while writing this book.

- **It is a principle of learning that people learn best when they do things.**
- **Many models of learning emphasise the importance of reflecting on and applying ideas as part of the learning process.**

Throughout the book there are reflective activities for you to complete. These often ask you to look at the ideas in the sections you have just read or to review your previous experience. They then ask you to apply them to your own context. You may choose to do these or not, but be aware that reading on its own is not an effective way of learning. Your brain needs to do things with new information, not simply acquire it. A parallel type of practice is asking students in a lecture to talk to their neighbours for two or three minutes about what they have just heard. The process is repeated three or four times during a one-hour lecture. This similarly increases retention and understanding.

You may find it helpful to keep a diary as you work through sections of the book. Keeping a diary is a good way of reflecting and planning. Some of the activities, especially at the end of chapters, suggest that you make some notes in your diary. Make your diary entries analytical rather than descriptive. Your diary would be particularly valuable if you were to maintain it when you put ideas into practice in your teaching.

You could keep your diary electronically in the form of a blog, a kind of electronic notepad for jotting down thoughts and ideas. If you wish, you can publish it on the internet for others to see and learn from your experiences and add comments. See Chapter 6 for some more detail on blogs.

- **Throughout the chapters I include teaching tips – more or less straightforward things for you to use in your teaching. You are investing some of your valuable time in reading this book. For that to be worthwhile, there ought to be some changes from which your learners benefit.**
- **Since one in three adults has a visual preference for information handling, I have included visual maps at the end of each chapter. I use a piece of software called MindManager to produce these maps. The map at the end of this chapter shows the main contents of the book.**

PRACTICAL TASK PRACTICAL TASK PRACTICAL TASK PRACTICAL TASK PRACTICAL TASK

Consider which is more helpful as an overview of what is in this book – the visual map at the end of this chapter or the table of contents at the start. Decide how you could use visual maps in your own teaching.

- The Lifelong Learning UK (LLUK) Standards are a map of the areas of teaching within which all Learning and Skills teachers work and are the basis for the compulsory Qualified Teacher Status Learning and Skills qualifications from September 2007. They refer on seven occasions to the use of new technology, but it is implicit throughout. For more detail, see Chapter 6.
- At the start of each chapter after this one is a reference to the LLUK Standards referencing new technology which are relevant to that chapter's content. They are also summarised in Table 1.1. Actually, if you look hard enough, you can probably find most of the Standards in most of the chapters – as you reflect on what you read in this book, see if you can find an e-learning way of carrying out each item of professional practice. You can download your own copy of the Standards from the LLUK website.
- At the end of each chapter you will find lists of further reading and websites to refer to if you want to follow up ideas raised in the chapter. This is an example of differentiation in practice. If you want to learn more, the opportunities are there. For clarity, I have avoided giving details of websites in the text, and collected them all together at the end of each chapter. The only exception to this is Chapter 8, where there are so many web references that it seemed easier to keep them with the text.
- Also at the end of each chapter is a signpost, which summarises what the chapter has covered and what the next chapter will explore. This is based on the learning principle that structuring information aids learning.

The reflective practitioner

The LLUK Standards and this book both use the model of the reflective practitioner. This is a model devised initially by Schön (1987) for professions such as nursing or social work where the job requires the application of skills, knowledge and understanding to situations that are unique. The situations are unique because people are involved, and people are unpredictable. Reflective practice is a process of continual improvement involving examining your experience to see what has happened, trying to make sense of it and then working out what to do next.

Reflective practice is the model behind most current teacher training courses. The whole point is to ensure that you can improve your practice and do it better next time. A helpful account of reflective practice is set out in Ashcroft and Foreman-Peck (1994).

REFLECTIVE TASK

Set up your diary or blog and then write a paragraph or two about what you hope to obtain by reading this book.

Chapter	2	3	4	5	6	7	8	9
Standard								
Domain B: Learning and teaching								
BP 3.1 Communicate effectively and appropriately using different forms of language and media, including written, oral and non verbal communication, and new and emerging technologies to enhance learning.		✓	✓	✓	✓	✓		✓
BP 5.1 Select and develop a range of effective resources, including appropriate use of new and emerging technologies.				✓	✓		✓	
Domain C: Specialist learning and teaching								
CK 3.5 Ways to support learners in the use of new and emerging technologies in own specialist area.			✓	✓				
CP 3.5 Make appropriate use of, and promote the benefits of new and emerging technologies.	✓		✓	✓	✓	✓		✓
Domain D: Planning for learning								
DP 1.2 Plan teaching sessions which meet the aims and needs of individual learners and groups, using a variety of resources, including new and emerging technologies.	✓	✓	✓	✓			✓	✓
Domain E: Assessment for learning								
EK 1.2 Ways to devise, select, use and appraise assessment tools, including where appropriate those which exploit new and emerging technologies.		✓	✓	✓		✓		
EP 1.2 Devise, select, use and appraise assessment tools, including where appropriate those which exploit new and emerging technologies.		✓	✓	✓				✓

Table 1.1 Coverage of the LLUK Standards

Visual overview

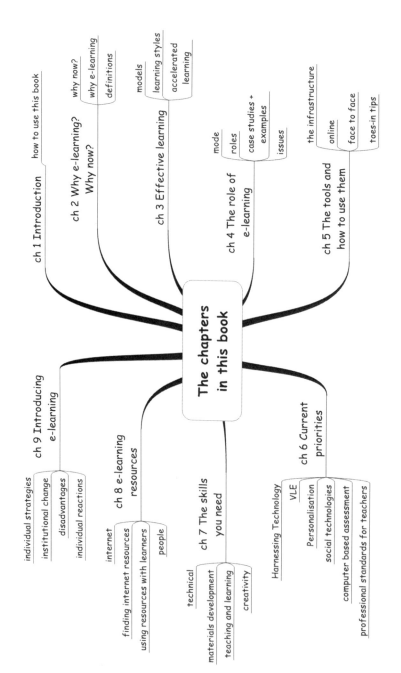

The chapters in this book

ch 1 Introduction — how to use this book

ch 2 Why e-learning? Why now?
- why now?
- why e-learning
- definitions

ch 3 Effective learning
- models
- learning styles
- accelerated learning

ch 4 The role of e-learning
- mode
- roles
- case studies + examples
- issues

ch 5 The tools and how to use them
- the infrastructure
- online
- face to face
- toes-in tips

ch 6 Current priorities
- Harnessing Technology
- VLE
- Personalisation
- social technologies
- computer based assessment
- professional standards for teachers

ch 7 The skills you need
- technical
- materials development
- teaching and learning
- creativity

ch 8 e-learning resources
- internet
- finding internet resources
- using resources with learners
- people

ch 9 Introducing e-learning
- individual strategies
- institutional change
- disadvantages
- individual reactions

This chapter has set out how this book is planned to work. How you actually use it is, of course, up to you. You might choose to read it in the sequence of the chapters or simply dip in and out.

In the next chapter we will start out by clarifying terms so that you can distinguish between IT, ICT, e-learning and ILT (among others), examine the current emphasis on ILT and e-learning and set out some of the benefits claimed for ILT. We will also consider research evidence trying to find out whether ILT actually makes a difference or not.

REFERENCES AND FURTHER READING REFERENCES AND FURTHER READING

Ashcroft, K. and Foreman-Peck, L. (1994) *Managing teaching and learning in further and higher education*. London: Falmer Press.

Schön, D. A. (1987) *Educating the reflective practitioner*. San Francisco: Jossey-Bass.

Websites

www.lsc.gov.uk The Learning and Skills Council website. You can also find your regional LSC through this site.

www.lluk.org Lifelong Learning UK is the Sector Skills Council responsible for the professional development of all those working in much of post-16 education and training.

http://whatis.techtarget.com An online dictionary of computing terms.

www.webopedia.com An alternative dictionary of computing.

2
Why e-learning? Why now?

This chapter will help you to:

- define and distinguish IT, ICT, ILT and e-learning;
- explain the current emphasis on ILT and e-learning;
- describe and explain the benefits that ILT and e-learning can provide.

LLUK Standards relevant to this chapter include:
CK3.5, CP3.5, DP1.2.

Many people enthuse about the contribution that the use of computer power can make to teaching and learning in colleges and other places where adults learn. Since 1998 the government has put considerable amounts of money into it. In December 1998 David Blunkett announced an allocation of £74 million over three years specifically for spending on information and learning technology (ILT) in the further education (FE) sector over and above the £300 million that the 428 colleges already planned to spend.

The spending continues. Between 2001 and 2007, the Learning and Skills Council (LSC) has spent over £260 million on the use of technology in teaching and learning in the sector. In August 2007, it announced it would invest a further £59.8 million in 2007–8 in new technology to improve the learner experience. This is an increase of £20 million on the previous year.

A whole herd of organisations support the developments, including the Joint Information Systems Committee (JISC), the British Educational Communication and Technology Agency (BECTA) and the Learning & Skills Network (LSN). JISC Regional Support Centres have been given extra funding to support learning providers in ACL and WBL in addition to the original colleges they supported. There are many initiatives and projects. Lots of people have taken on new jobs both locally and nationally. All sorts of people in all sorts of learning providers have been required to produce Information Learning Technology strategies and to update them since. Obviously someone thinks it is important.

Definitions

To start off, let's define our terms. We are in fact only getting to the point where agreement on the use of terms is emerging. In this book I will use the definitions proposed by BECTA: don't be surprised if you come across different ones elsewhere. (See Powell, Knight and Smith, 2003.)

The kit on its own is *information technology* (IT). This might be a standalone computer with any number of accessories to go with it such as scanner or printer. It might be job-specific computers such as the one found in many modern car engines or in a computer-controlled lathe.

It might be the electronic musical keyboard with a built-in facility to record tunes. Word processing a document is an example of using IT.

When you link up pieces of kit, you get *information and communications technology* (ICT). ICT is the connecting together of IT hardware either within an organisation or beyond it. Surfing the internet and online banking are examples of using ICT.

Neither of these definitions puts any emphasis on what the computer technology is used for. When the IT/ICT is used to support what learning providers are there for – getting students onto and through courses where they learn effectively – the concept becomes *information and learning technology* (ILT). BECTA defines ILT as:

> *the application of IT/ICT to the core business of colleges – learning and teaching – as well as the management of the learning environment and business systems that support and enable effective learning.* (Powell, Knight and Smith, 2003, p4)

So what is *e-learning*? It is 'those parts of ILT which directly support effective learning and teaching' (ibid. p4). In other words, it focuses on the use of IT/ICT for teaching and learning but excludes the business uses of IT/ICT, such as electronic enrolment of students or electronic registers.

Markos Tiris suggested that the relationship between the terms might be shown diagrammatically as a series of overlapping ellipses, as set out in Figure 2.1 (Powell, Knight and Smith, 2003).

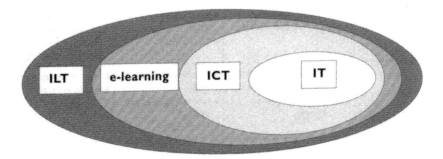

Figure 2.1 The relationship between IT, ICT, e-learning and ILT

This shows the scale of the terms. The overall concept is information and learning technology which contains e-learning. These two both contain the idea of purpose, what the kit is used for. The most restricted concept is IT: IT is the kit and ICT is the kit joined together. Neither IT nor ICT contains any idea of purpose.

Teaching tip

What is the visual message that this diagram gives? As well as the way that I have described it, does it give the visual message that IT is at the centre and e-learning and ILT are peripheral? This is exactly the opposite message to the one intended. When you use diagrams (and you should do so frequently because many learners have a visual preference), consider the visual message they give.

This book is about ILT but has a particular focus on e-learning. Throughout I will do my best to be precise in my use of the terms. If you are not yet clear as to the distinctions, don't worry. You are not alone: many managers and practitioners in the Learning and Skills sector feel the same. Incidentally, only the further education sector uses the term 'Information and Learning Technology', which comes from the 1996 Higginson Report (FEFC, 1996). For other people the initials ILT stand for many different things. Table 2.1 summarises the differences.

Term	Definition	Skills needed	Example of use by a teacher
IT	computer hardware and software	• skills to use the kit and its specific applications	• prepare a word-processed handout
ICT	computers linked together to form networks	• skills to use the communications facilities	• search for material on the internet • send e-mails
e-learning	computing applied to teaching and learning	• teaching and learning skills • IT/ICTskills	• tutoring online • students make PowerPoint presentations
ILT	computing applied to the whole business of further education colleges	• teaching and learning skills • learner management skills	• electronic registers • online enrolment

Table 2.1 Definitions, skills and examples

Table 2.1 shows the development of the skills needed in each of the four settings. In one way that is a bit scary for those of us trying to work in information and learning technology: ILT demands an impressive range of skills. It is probably much more encouraging to see the wider range of skills needed in e-learning and ILT as something really positive. Teachers are required to have teaching and learning skills and learner management skills already and all you need to do is to build in the IT/ICT aspect. In other words, teachers have most of the skills already – and by far the most important ones.

PRACTICAL TASK PRACTICAL TASK PRACTICAL TASK PRACTICAL TASK PRACTICAL TASK

Draw up a list of your own uses of computing, both in education and the rest of your life. Decide which of them are IT, which ICT, which e-learning and which ILT.

But what exactly is e-learning?

Our definition of e-learning – those parts of ICT that directly support effective learning and teaching – is accurate but diverse. What might it mean in practice? If you were a student learning by e-learning, what would it be like? Here are some examples, and you will see that they are very different.

Example I: AS classical civilisation

In this full-time AS level classical civilisation class, learning is organised in traditional face-to-face sessions. There is access to a single computer and data projector. Sometimes it is used by the tutor to deliver short PowerPoint presentations (no more than ten minutes) but, more frequently, it is used by the students for presentations they have prepared either individually or in small groups. The tutor has also collected together onto a CD pictures she has taken and they too will be projected at relevant points in the sessions. A good cataloguing system means that the tutor is able to call up relevant images in response to topics that emerge in discussion.

Example 2: Certificate in Teaching, Learning and Skills

This group is working towards the mandatory qualification for all FE teachers. They meet once a week. Most course members hold down full-time or part-time jobs so the chance to meet other than in the class sessions is very limited. In between the taught sessions, course members are required to take part in online discussion run over the internet. Two-thirds of the class can do this from home, but other course members have to find internet access elsewhere, such as in the local library. Some course members come into college when they can to use the free internet facilities there. There is a website that supports the course. From it, course members can obtain the forms they need; for example, session plans. The site also contains a variety of learning material and links to internet sites that course members are free to browse.

Example 3: NVQ in management

These learners are all based in the workplace.There are no taught classes but learners work on a one-to-one basis with a tutor who supports them in the construction of a portfolio of evidence and then assesses it. Learners may be based up to 50 miles away from the college. Before a tutorial, the learner e-mails the tutor with a draft of their evidence statement so that the tutor can read it in readiness for the tutorial. The assessment is recorded in the workplace using a laptop computer and a piece of specialist software.

Example 4: Chartered Institute of Purchasing and Supply

Here whole modules of the course are delivered entirely online with no face-to-face sessions at all. Learners, who may be scattered throughout the country or abroad, can enrol on and complete each module at any time although exams are only held on fixed dates each year. The course is available 24 hours a day for seven days a week. Everything is done online – materials delivered, assessments conducted, tutorials given. The tutor is able to track when learners have been online and what they have done. The only thing that is not done online is enrolment, because the college maintains that it needs a course members signature.

These examples, while very different, all fall within our definition of e-learning. We will explore in Chapter 4 a classification of the different types of e-learning.

Why now?

In this section we explore what has caused the current emphasis on e-learning.

Developing technology

From the mid twentieth century, most aspects of society moved significantly towards exploiting the power of the microchip. This is not only in the personal computer but ranges from the programmes on a washing machine, through hole-in-the-wall cash machines, to online shopping and the mobile phone. It is no surprise that the same is true of education and training. More or less enthusiastic teachers have creatively adapted the technology to the learning context and specific applications have been developed for education and training use.

Expectations

Because learners, teachers and managers live in an information society, they come to learning with the expectation that computers will be used there too. There is an expectation that all teachers are ICT literate; many learning providers include ICT competence in the person specification for lecturer jobs. *Equipping our Teachers for the Future* (DfES 2004), the DfES document setting out the strategy for initial teacher training, requires that the core skills for all teachers 'must include the skills for using e-learning'.

Some of the strongest pressure comes from students asking 'this tutor puts stuff online for us – why don't you?'

Government support

In the further education sector, the current impetus comes from the 1996 Higginson Report for the Further Education Funding Council, the body through which funding for FE was channelled before the Learning and Skills Council (LSC) was established. This report set out a picture for the use of information technology to support learning in colleges, and many of the developments that have taken place since reflect its recommendations.

A technical difficulty with Higginson's recommendations was that no money was provided at the time to make them happen. The money materialised in 1998 soon after the election of the Labour government. Since then much has been achieved. In his presentation to the ILT Champions Conference held in Derby in February 2002, Bob Powell, at that time Head of Lifelong Learning at BECTA, identified three crucial achievements, backed up by evidence from the annual BECTA survey of ILT in colleges, which is where the figures in the following paragraphs come from.

- *The physical infrastructure is in place*. Using a network called JANET, all colleges have a direct high-speed (now usually 10 megabit) link to the internet. Many ACL managing agents are also connected. The target of having one computer for every five full time students in colleges was achieved as early as 2001 (1:4.95 full time equivalent students in 2001) and the target of one computer for every permanent member of staff has nearly been met (1:1.9 in 2001).
- *There are appropriate management structures in place*. In order to ensure that the introduction of ILT was well thought through, mainstream and specialist colleges and ACL have been required to capture their plans in an ILT Strategy. The same approach is being commended to WBL. Many learning providers have updated their ILT strategies; others have chosen not to have a separate strategy but to embed (that's a word that will keep cropping up) it in other strategies, such as the learning strategy.

- *The original model for change used ILT Champions.* The original plan was for one Management Champion and one Curriculum Champion in each college but the BECTA survey shows that the typical college at one point had three Champions. The Champions were not technical people: they champion in the sense of being enthusiasts, even evangelists, for ILT. At one point, 92 per cent of colleges had Champions, although the gloss is taken off the picture a bit by the fact that 31 per cent of the Champions had no time allocated to do the job. Many colleges have maintained the Champion model and it has also spread to ACL and WBL in the form of e-guides. What Champions actually do varies from place to place, but it is recognised that the Champion pattern is successful in changing classroom practice, much more so for example than models used in school teacher e-learning training.

	Organisation	Roles include	Website
BECTA	British Educational Communications and Technology Agency	• focuses on strategic role of ILT	www.becta.org.uk
LSN	Learning and Skills Network	• quality and staff development programmes	www.lsneducation.org.uk
JISC	Joint Information Systems Committee	• providing advisory and support services, for example TechDis and the Plagiarism service • providing the nine Regional Support Centres • channel for funding innovative projects	www.jisc.ac.uk
NILTA	National Information and Learning Technology Association	• part of the Association of Colleges • member organisation enabling the exchange of ideas, expertise and practice	www.nilta.org.uk
QIA	Quality Improvement Agency	• hosts the Excellence gateway website	www.qia.org.uk
RSCs	Regional Support Centres	• strategic and operational support • regional events and networks • support to individual learning providers	www.jisc.ac.uk/rsc
JANET (UK)	Joint Academic Network (formerly UKERNA)	• manages and develops develops the high speed broadband network linking all colleges and universities	www.ja.net

Table 2.2 Partners in external support

- *There is a framework for external support*. There are several key organisations formally involved in supporting ILT in the Learning and Skills Sector, set out in Table 2.2. At one time they were in a formal partnership called the National Learning Network (NLN), but now the partnership is less formal but still effective.

The three achievements that Bob Powell identifies are remarkable. Do not underestimate them. In much of the Learning and Skills sector a good platform for development has been established. We have the kit, the management structure and the external support framework. All we have to do now is to use them to make a difference to the experience our learners have.

The advantages of e-learning

Much of the thrust towards e-learning comes from the fact that teachers and those who make decisions about education believe it gives advantages not available otherwise. The next section explores some of these.

PRACTICAL TASK PRACTICAL TASK PRACTICAL TASK PRACTICAL TASK PRACTICAL TASK

What do you think are the main advantages of using e-learning? Make a list. Decide whether the advantage is mainly for the learner, mainly for the tutor or for both. Compare your answer with my ideas in the following section.

Why use e-learning?

There are many claimed advantages for e-learning, although the reality may be somewhat different. Later on we will look at some of the research evidence for the effectiveness of e-learning, but first here is the case for using e-learning. Because e-learning takes many different forms, not all the advantages listed here apply in every setting.

Teaching tip

Encourage your learners to be sceptical of everything they read on the internet (and anywhere else for that matter). Make a mantra of the phrase 'Who says so and how do they know?' I hope, too, that you adopt a little healthy scepticism to what you read in this book.

- Classroom learning is accessed at a specific time and place, although it would be silly to say that learning only takes place within that classroom. By contrast, much e-learning can be accessed at any time and in any location where the kit is available. This means that learning is much more accessible to the many potential learners excluded because they work shifts, live in remote locations or have conflicting commitments. Learners learn when the time is right for them.
- There are real barriers to accessing traditional learning for some learners, especially those who have not been successful in the educational system and have low expectations of achievement. E-learning may be able to break down the stigma felt by some of these groups of learners to improve inclusion and participation.
- It is one of my beliefs as a teacher that most people can learn most things, but it takes some of us longer to get there than others. So the opportunity that e-learning gives for learners to learn at their

own pace is a real strength. In a face-to-face class the teacher may feel forced to work at an 'average' speed that is too fast for some and too slow for others. With e-learning, each learner controls their own rate of working and can revisit sections they find difficult.

- E-learning can meet different learning styles. Different learners like to learn differently. With e-learning, learners can be given choices enabling activities and format to be customised for them. Choices might include reading text on a screen or listening to it being spoken; working through material in a linear fashion or exploring in a more random order; annotating a digital image or producing a written description. Some learners have more specific learning needs, such as voice recognition for those who find writing difficult.
- Computers now have considerable potential both in the use of multimedia and for interaction. The use of graphics, video and audio with different input and output devices means that more of our senses can be stimulated by e-learning. If more senses are used, more learning is likely to take place, although you may well have seen examples of too much stimulation. (If you can stand it, have a look at the 'websitesthatsuck' website.) People learn more when they do things, not simply gaze at a screen passively. We are getting much better at building into e-learning interactions which take the learner's attention.

The advantages above accrue mainly to the student, but e-learning gives advantages to the tutor and the institution providing the course, too.

- It is often claimed that e-learning is cheaper per learner than traditional training. However, there is relatively little evidence for this. The experience of many learning providers is that e-learning needs tutor support to be effective, and tutor support is costly. The tutor gives attention, encouragement, feedback and flexibility and shows the learner that he or she is important. Where e-learning may well be cheaper is in the costs other than the course fee that the learner pays – what an economist would call externalities, the costs other than price passed on by the producer to the consumer. In particular, for a face-to-face course, the learner has to pay travel costs and may well miss out on income because of attending a class at a time when they might work. Against this must be balanced the cost the learner pays to buy their own home computer and the cost of connecting to the internet.
- E-learning can be much more scalable. If you want to double the number of learners going through a classroom-based course, you need two of everything – room, tutor, materials – and the cost accordingly doubles. In an e-learning course costs do rise as learner numbers rise, but not as quickly. As a result there are economies of scale. The initial cost of preparing an online course (i.e. a course to be delivered over the internet or a computer network) is greater than that of a traditional course, but it costs relatively little more to deliver online to 300 learners than to deliver to 30. Many of the things that take much of a tutor's time in a traditional class can be done by the computer; for example, marking. Tutoring costs will rise as more learners are enrolled, but not proportionally. It takes a tutor no longer to send a group e-mail to 60 people than to five.
- In traditional teaching, many of us re-invent the wheel each time we teach a subject. With e-learning, the course is retained from one group to the next. In fact, where evaluations take place each time a course runs, the course will be continually improved. It will also be consistent: each student will get a broadly similar experience.
- E-learning delivery often involves a mechanism for automatically tracking what the student is doing. For example, many e-learning courses are delivered using a virtual learning environment (VLE), which is a collection of tools designed for learning (see Chapter 5 on tools). A VLE will tell the tutor which students have logged on, when, how long they spent online, which pages they visited, what scores they achieved in tests and what they said in discussions. In fact, the tutor is likely to get far more information than is needed.
- E-learning material is designed in such away that it can be used in different courses. In e-learning, subject material is broken down into small chunks. When one of these chunks is attached to an objective (what the learner will be able to do when they have finished the chunk) and an assessment to check whether they can do it or not, it becomes what is called a learning object, as shown in Figure 2.2.

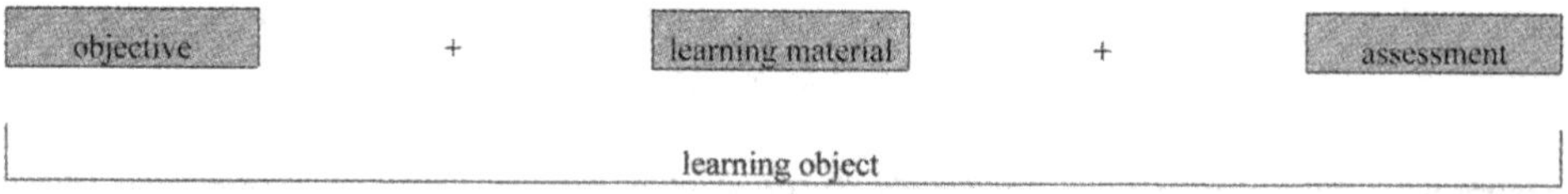

Figure 2.2 A learning object

One learning object may be used in many different courses. For example, in the materials produced for free distribution by the National Learning Network there is a learning object about the colour wheel. It was initially designed for students on horticulture courses. However, exactly the same object can be used on any course where learners need to be able to use colours together – floristry, art and design, hair and beauty, interior decoration, web page design, etc. To ensure it can be used in several different settings, the learning object must be produced to a standard, but once you have a collection of appropriate objects it does make course design a much simpler process of selecting objects from a library.

- Probably the strongest pedagogical argument for e-learning is that it frees the tutor for higher-level activity. By contrast, in a formal lecture, the lecturer only has opportunity to deliver information. There is little chance to get to know individual learners, to give them significant feedback, to diagnose their learning needs and to vary the learning process accordingly. In e-learning, however, many of the routine aspects of teaching such as delivering information and organising learner activity are carried out by the computer, leaving the teacher free to concentrate on the learner and the learning.

Some research evidence

Do you believe these arguments? They certainly seem plausible to me. However, when I looked for rigorous research evidence to back up the claims, it is relatively thin on the ground.

In 2002, Jill Attewell, Research Manager for the Learning and Skills Development Agency, reviewed research on the use and effectiveness of distributed and electronic learning (DEL) in post-compulsory education and training (LSDA, 2002). This was in a project on behalf of the Learning and Skills Council (LSC), the body which is the main channel for government funding into post-16 education and training. Attewell identified more than 500 research documents from the internet and concludes that 'few studies have produced substantial evidence of the "effectiveness" of DEL', which is not what the LSC was looking for.

The research review shows that it is hard to be definite. Much of the research is small scale and qualitative, focusing on the experience of particular groups of learners. Individually these studies may not be reliable, but together they add up to useful evidence. It is also complicated by the fact that the benefits apparently resulting from e-learning actually come more from the move to learner-centred approaches that is also taking place.

Among the key findings are the following.

- DEL can improve access to learning and learning support, learner motivation, achievement, and participation in lifelong learning.
- Educators and policymakers have faith in the benefits of ILT.
- Online and face-to-face tutoring are key factors in the success of DEL.
- Some experimental studies showed worse retention than in the traditional learning control group.
- In workplace training, DEL has shown that it can train more employees more quickly, reduce off-the-job time and result in better knowledge retention.
- Not all e-learning is designed with the requirements of learners with disabilities and learning difficulties in mind.

Four critical success factors are identified.

- DEL is used to help build confidence, increase motivation and learning (and not only subject knowledge).
- Technology is chosen to suit the achievement of the learning objectives rather than adapting learning to suit the technology.
- A well-structured approach is used, proceeding incrementally and allowing for progression.
- Individual and group learning styles and preferences are considered.

(LSDA, 2002, p2)

Obtain a copy of the review and explore its ideas. It is worth doing as it covers such a broad sweep.

REFLECTIVE TASK

Look back at the ideas about the move towards e-learning in this chapter. Write a paragraph or so in your diary or on your own blog about how realistic you think the claims made about it are.

SIGNPOST In this chapter we have set out where the momentum towards e-learning comes from and some of the claims made about it. We have seen that the claims have yet to be fully substantiated. Is e-learning simply another educational fashion that will, in due course, be replaced?

In the next chapter we will concentrate on how the learning process works and explore how e-learning links to the learning process.

Visual overview

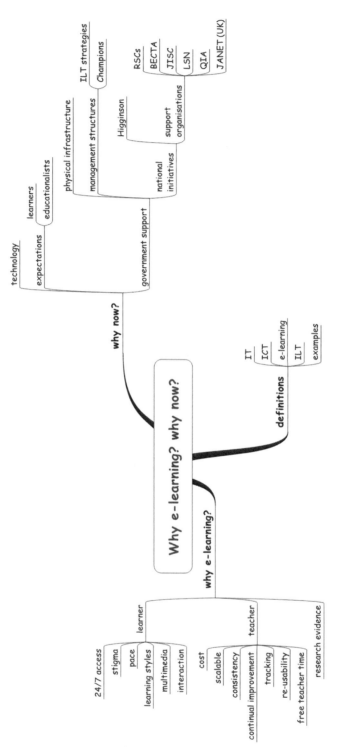

REFERENCES AND FURTHER READING REFERENCES AND FURTHER READING

DfES (2004) *Equipping our teachers for the future* available online at www.dfes.gov.uk Enter the title in the site's search box (accessed 6 June 2007).

FEFC (1996) *Report of the FEFC Learning & Technology Committee* (Higginson Report) currently out of print.

LSDA (2002) *Distributed and electronic learning: a review of the literature* Project number RPM 449 available online at www.lsneducation.org.uk. Follow the publications link and search by the publication number (accessed 6 June 2007).

Powell, B., Knight, S. and Smith, R. (2003) *Managing inspection and ILT* BECTA available online at http://ferl.qia.org.uk. Enter the title in the site's search engine (accessed 6 June 2007).

Websites

qia.org.uk It is possible to download the ILT Champion training material from the FERL part of the Excellence Gateway website. Enter 'champions' in the site's search facility.

www.nln.ac.uk The National Learning Network website originally linked the work of all the NLN partners and their facilities. Now it focuses on the online materials produced by that initiative.

www.websitesthatsuck.com Learn what makes a good website by looking at some really appalling ones.

3
Effective learning

This chapter will help you to:

- **explain how e-learning relates to some models of learning;**
- **explore how e-learning helps to meet individual learning styles.**

LLUK Standards relevant to this chapter include:
BP3.1, DP1.2, EK1.2, EP1.2.

This is a book about learning, not about technology. The better our understanding of learning, the more successful we can be in bringing it about. In this chapter, you will explore some ways of looking at learning so that you can make your use of e-learning effective.

Teaching tip

Teach your learners about the learning process so that they understand why you ask them to do the things you do. Remember, learning is a skill and, like any skill, it can be developed by practice.

PRACTICAL TASK PRACTICAL TASK PRACTICAL TASK PRACTICAL TASK PRACTICAL TASK

In this activity you reflect on the things you believe are important in learning. Complete the following sentence in at least ten different ways:

'People learn best when...'

From your list, pick out what you believe to be the three most important conditions for effective learning. What is true in traditional learning is also true in e-learning.

There are many different models explaining how learning happens. I have chosen ones that fit with the experience of my course members and that make sense to me. The key point is that each model through its perspective enables us to improve our practice as teachers.

Model I: Ripples in a pond

Race (Ellington, Percival and Race, 1993) identifies four things that people report as significant in their experience of learning. He likens them to ripples spreading outwards from a stone dropped into a pond, set out in Figure 3.1.

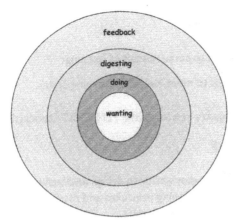

Figure 3.1 Ripples in a pond model

Wanting

At the centre of his model is wanting to learn. If learners do not want to learn, limited learning will take place. People may want to learn for many different reasons, both intrinsic (for example, interest in the subject) and extrinsic (for example, to obtain a qualification which might lead to a better job and higher income). They may want to learn because they need to learn.

Doing

People learn best when they are doing things, when they are active rather than passive. Lectures are a relatively inefficient way of learning because it is too easy for learners to be passive in them. When I am observing a class delivered by one of my teachers in training, my criteria include asking myself how easy it would be for a learner in the class to sit and do nothing – and in a surprising number of classes learners can be inactive throughout.

Digesting

Learners need the opportunity to digest new ideas – to use them, to play with them, to see how they fit with what is already known and to construct a new understanding. As teachers, we arrange activities for our learners where they can apply the ideas to new settings, and where they can use them to solve problems.

Feedback

Feedback is crucial to learning. When learners feel they are being successful, they are encouraged to learn more. Hattie (1999), Professor of Education at New Zealand's Auckland University, has reviewed 180,000 studies to identify what has the greatest effect on student learning, covering over 50 million students. He identifies reinforcement as by far the strongest factor. It has an effect equivalent to improving the rate of learning by over 50 per cent. Does every single one of your learners get some positive feedback in every single learning session you run?

PRACTICAL TASK PRACTICAL TASK PRACTICAL TASK PRACTICAL TASK PRACTICAL TASK

Consider how each of the components in the 'ripples in a pond' model relates to e-learning. Compare your ideas with those in the following section.

The 'ripples in a pond' model and e-learning

Can e-learning encourage *wanting to* learn? Certainly some learners find using a computer attractive. Other people will be intimidated by the thought of e-learning, especially if they have not tried e-learning before and believe the skills will be difficult to learn.

- Motivation is strengthened when learners believe that they are learning successfully. Well designed e-learning material is broken down into small chunks and completion of each section can give a regular and frequent sense of achievement, which encourages the learner to keep going.
- Including audio and video enables material to be intrinsically much more interesting.
- Being able to access e-learning from home at a convenient time is much more attractive than having to travel miles to your class on a cold, wet Tuesday evening.

Well designed e-learning gets learners *doing* lots of different things. In a simulation of the UK economy a student of economics might play the role of Chancellor of the Exchequer. The student can make decisions about taxes – which tax to alter, whether to raise or lower it and by how much – and the computer will work out the consequences for the economy. A student on a social care course might be presented by a series of potential clients created on computer by a 'random person generator' and be asked to decide how best to support each client. E-learning can keep learners active by building in such opportunities for interaction as choosing between options, problem solving and taking part in simulations.

E-learning can build in many opportunities for *digesting*. Online discussions enable learners to capture and clarify ideas simply by inputting them through the keyboard. Learners who would find it difficult to join in with a face-to-face discussion are often more able to express opinions online when they have the chance to think what they want to say first. Digesting takes time and is often not a conscious process. With an asynchronous discussion, the learner can contribute when the light dawns.

E-learning makes it possible for learners to get more frequent, individualised *feedback*. In a traditional classroom, unless students are asked to mark their own work, the teacher has to do the marking. Personally, I feel that spending hours on my own marking student work is a very unproductive use of my time, but it is very different if the student is with me. E-learning has a range of assessment tools that not only give the student feedback but also record the results for the teacher to monitor. Virtual learning environments contain assessment tools, or there are stand-alone programs such as Hot Potatoes and Question Mark.

Teaching tip

Get your learners to construct short multiple-choice tests for you. Constructing the questions will make the learners think as much as answering them. Each test could contain five or six questions. Store the tests in an archive the learners can access. Make sure each test has a name that makes it easy to identify.

Model 2: Experiential learning

Kolb (1984) suggests a model of learning based on a cycle of learning from experience, as set out in Figure 3.2.

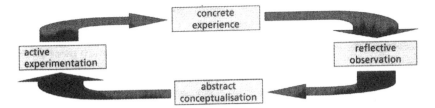

Figure 3.2 The Kolb experiential learning model

Kolb emphasises the importance of experience for learning, both real experience and second-hand experience such as simulation. This he refers to as concrete experience. However, it is not enough to have an experience. To learn from it, you need to reflect on the experience that you have – reflective observation. Do you find you make the same mistake over and over again? Could this be because you haven't reflected on it? Once you are aware of what happens, you can then make sense of it by considering why it happens – abstract conceptualisation. You can then test out your understanding by predicting what will happen when you apply it to a new situation – active experimentation. Figure 3.3 expresses the model in more familiar terms.

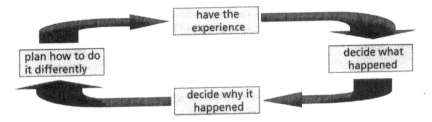

Figure 3.3 The Kolb model rephrased

In learning, the concrete experience might be experience of a practical skill or an academic activity such as analysing a historical situation.

Teaching tip

Traditional teaching tends to focus on abstract conceptualisation – often in the form of a lecture, or reading a book – and concrete experience. Reflective observation and active experimentation often get overlooked. Aim to include them. Include diaries and observation sheets to encourage reflection: get learners to devise an action plan or draw up a list of assessment criteria for a skill they are to perform as a way of encouraging application.

PRACTICAL TASK PRACTICAL TASK PRACTICAL TASK PRACTICAL TASK PRACTICAL TASK

Think about the teaching and learning strategies you use. Which of the stages in the Kolb model do your strategies mainly fall into?

An e-learning example applying the experiential learning model

When you are designing e-learning, you should also try to apply the experiential learning cycle. In a customer care course, learners learn how to deal with a dissatisfied customer. Table 3.1 is an example of how e-learning might contribute to that in the context of the experiential learning model. The example uses a blend of e-learning and traditional learning. It starts with preparatory work done online before a face-to-face session, which is followed by further e-learning activity.

Stage in the cycle	Activity
reflective observation	In groups of 6–8, learners contribute to an online discussion describing examples of their own experience of being a dissatisfied customer.
abstract conceptualisation	Based on the contributions, each group member identifies the three most common causes of dissatisfaction and sends them to one group member, who combines them into an overall list and allocates causes to pairs of group members.
active experimentation	Each pair suggests appropriate strategies to cope with the causes of dissatisfaction they have been allocated.
concrete experience	In the face-to-face session, group members role-play different scenarios. Role plays are video-recorded: digital recordings can be viewed through a computer and stored for access later.
reflective observation	Videos are reviewed to find strategies that work: findings are developed and recorded using software that composes visual maps.
abstract conceptualisation	Internet research to identify customers' legal rights over return of goods.
active experimentation	Using a word-processor or desktop publishing package, learners individually make a guidance booklet on how to deal with dissatisfied customers.

Table 3.1 An example of e-learning and the Kolb cycle

In this example, e-learning contributes at every stage.

PRACTICAL TASK PRACTICAL TASK PRACTICAL TASK PRACTICAL TASK PRACTICAL TASK

For a topic that you teach, work out a sequence of activities following the stages of the experiential learning cycle. Where might e-learning contribute? Set it out on a copy of the Kolb diagram.

Model 3: Deep and surface learning

A very helpful distinction is that between deep and surface learning (Ashcroft and Foreman-Peck, 1994). Surface learning is about remembering, often for the short term.

Deep learning is about understanding, getting inside a subject and making sense of it. Surface learning is not an effective way to learn but many learners can identify examples of it in their previous educational experience. For example, some of us learned to carry out mathematical calculations by mechanically chanting multiplication tables rather than understanding what was going on.

Be wary of some computer 'tutorials' that come with commercial applications packages. They can simply present information, albeit in a glossy, multimedia way, and as such tend towards surface learning. In the same way that there is still a place for the face-to-face lecture – provided it doesn't go on for more than 15 minutes – there is a place for creative presentation of information in e-learning, but it has to be part of an overall package that keeps the learner busy and gives time to digest ideas.

Teaching tip

'Death by PowerPoint' is not a pleasant way to go, so don't do it. Instead, get your learners to devise their own PowerPoint mini-presentations of no more than five slides – it makes them think much more, which is the basis of deep learning. Keep the presentations in an archive that other learners can access and ask later leavers to evaluate and improve on the work of their predecessors.

Model 4: Accelerated learning – whole-brain learning

Smith (1996) points out that 80 per cent of our knowledge about how the brain works in learning has emerged over the past 15 years. As a result, there has been a whole raft of strategies for learning based on our new understanding. These strategies focus on using the whole brain for learning and collectively are called accelerated learning.

Although our understanding of how the brain works is continuing to develop, the key aspects that underpin accelerated learning are as follows.

Connections

The brain depends for its learning power on connections between the brain cells (neurons). Since the average person starts off with 100 billion brain cells and each brain cell can have up to 20,000 branches (dendrites, meaning 'tree like') which make the connections, the average brain is anything but average in its potential. When neurons are stimulated in learning, connections are made between neurons, at first electrically and then chemically. This fits with what our experience of learning tells us.

- **Learning needs reinforcement (connections strengthened).**
- **What people know already is a key factor in learning (new connections link to existing connections).**
- **We forget (connections not well established).**
- **Most significantly, our learning potential is not fixed (more connections!).**

Three-part brain

Different parts of the brain have different functions and they all have direct implications for learning.

- The reptilian brain, at the top of the spinal cord, looks after many basic functions including breathing and heart rate. If we feel threatened, this is the part of the brain that responds initially. If we feel threatened, we are unlikely to learn very much.
- The limbic system is in many ways the control centre of the brain. It is also where emotions and long-term memory are based. Emotions are strongly linked to learning: 'People learn in direct proportion to the amount of fun they are having' (Bob Pike of Creative Training Techniques, quoted in Rose and Nicholl (1997)).
- The neo-cortex deals with rational thought, creating, decision making and the senses. The more senses that are stimulated, the more effective learning is likely to be.

Left brain–right brain

The left side of the brain is more concerned with language, logic, linear progression and analytical thinking. The right side is more concerned with rhyme, rhythm, pattern and the whole picture.

So what does all this mean for learning if we are to mobilise the whole brain? Here are some strategies for implementing accelerated learning in any teaching. Afterwards we will apply these ideas to e-learning.

- **Create a good environment for learning.** Make it relaxed and stress-free, perhaps with background music. Apparently baroque music – which is often very rhythmic and regular – is the best, although your learners may have other tastes. Personally, I recommend Ella Fitzgerald, Spirogyra or Hugh Masekela. Sometimes a good environment just happens but if you want to be sure there is a good environment, you have to work at creating it.
- **Stimulate both left and right brain.** Include a mix of activities – for example, something logical such as sorting steps into order, combined with something that involves more lateral thinking such as problem solving. A geographer studying land use might use maps to look for patterns in where the industrial areas are in several British towns – right brain – and calculate from statistical information where the cheapest place for a firm to locate is – left brain.
- **Use the whole array of senses** so the learner is using more of their brain power. Include plenty of variety in the learning experience. Stimulate the learner's sight (for example, with pictures and video), sound (speech and sound effects) and touch (sorting decision cards). You can even use taste and smell, for example by associating successful learning with pleasant experiences such as the smell of new bread or the taste of chocolate.
- **Look at the whole picture.** It is important that the learner can see the whole picture as well as the part they are working on.
- **Create mind maps.** Mind maps are an excellent way to set out the concepts that relate to an idea. Teach your students how to draw them. Include colour and graphics to exploit the visual. Use them at the start of a topic to give an overview, throughout a topic to provide the framework for ideas, and at the end of the topic for summary and revision.
- **Frequently review the learning that is taking place.** Look at what has recently been learned to see that it makes sense and to understand how it all fits together. Learning is a process of fitting new ideas into what is known already and reviewing is a key part of doing this.
- **Encourage your learners to put the new learning into words.** Articulating the knowledge reinforces the connections between neurons. Putting things into words means that learners have to have a clear idea of what they are trying to say. Making learners think about the words to use helps them clarify their understanding – or at least highlights the parts they do not understand.
- **Make learning fun** – it helps the brain work more efficiently. Be creative and original. Encourage learners to smile. Collect jokes to do with your subject. Even computing, which is not noted for humour, has built-in jokes – did you know that half a byte is called a nibble?

> **Teaching tip**
>
> Present information to your learners as mini-lectures that last no more than ten minutes. At the end of that time, resolve any issues that need clarifying, then give learners five minutes to teach a partner the same ideas. After five minutes the partner teaches the same material back.

How do we apply these strategies to e-learning?

Environment
If the e-learning is done in comfortable surroundings at home, the learner is much more likely to be relaxed. However, at home, there will be distractions such as children and *Coronation Street* which interrupt and frustrate the learner. Music helps, although my experience is that background music doesn't work with musicians – they insist on listening to it. Make sure your learners have regular breaks to freshen the mind. Encourage them to sip water.

Online communication can feel impersonal because it excludes many communication elements such as tone of voice, gesture and facial expression. Use each learner's name frequently and make sure each learner receives some personal communication and is not just included in group e-mails. You need to create an environment where learners do not feel threatened. A good test is to ask yourself how worried your learners would be about making a mistake. Good software design minimises any fears of the technology that your learners may have, but your tutoring skills are more important in developing a non-threatening atmosphere where learners learn from errors they make. It might be as straightforward as sending a friendly e-mail to the relevant learner.

Left and right brain
Computing itself is a combination of the logical and the creative. Some aspects make the user pay attention to detail and to carry out operations in a specific order – try entering a website address that is not completely accurate. On the other hand, there are often many ways to do the same thing: how many different ways of centring a heading in Microsoft Word can you think of? Can you beat the six I came up with in two minutes? More significantly, Word was designed for office use, not learning, yet it has many features that you can use with your learners, such as comments boxes to give hints or drop-down boxes in Forms to create multiple-choice tests. Show your learners how to create text boxes and use them to annotate diagrams. You are only limited by your imagination.

All the senses
Take advantage of the developing multimedia power of the computer. Do not simply have pages of text for your learners to read – when you buy software for your learners, don't just look for pictures and text but audio and video too. Set your learners tasks that involve them not just writing text but incorporating pictures they have taken with the digital camera or downloaded from the internet, and speech they record directly using a microphone attached to the computer's sound card.

The whole picture
As well as designing the sequence of learning so that it starts from the big picture, focuses in on the individual parts and frequently returns to the overview, build in opportunities for your learners to explain how their new understanding fits with what they already know. Using mind maps is an excellent way to do this.

Mind maps

Freemind, Mindmanager and Mindgenius are examples of specialist mindmapping software available for drawing mind maps which are visually effective and simple to use. Freemind is open source software which means that it is free and open to anyone with the inclination, skills and energy to improve it. You can download it from the Sourceforge website. If your students do not have access to mindmapping software, get them to draw mind maps by hand and then scan them in so they can be easily distributed. If you have access to an interactive whiteboard, capture the maps that way.

Review the learning

Give learners lots of opportunities to go back over material they have studied and to stop and take stock every so often. This is much easier when the learner has access when they want and the learning materials have a decent navigation/indexing system. Build in frequent self-marking assessments so the learner is getting feedback on their understanding.

Put the learning into words

Ask your learners to write out their new understanding as text, present it as a PowerPoint presentation, explain it to each other in e-mails or record a short audio clip.

Make learning fun

Include animations and graphics in web pages. Celebrate good things that your learners do in an online gallery. Look for the original and creative in internet sites.

Model 5: Multiple intelligence

Gardner's multiple intelligence model is complementary to the ideas of accelerated learning and is usually included in accelerated learning books and courses (Rose and Nicholl, 1997). Gardner explores the idea of intelligence, which he defines as 'an ability to solve a problem or fashion a product that is valued in one or more cultural settings'. It is certainly much more than what is measured by conventional intelligence tests. In reality, intelligence tests only measure the ability to be successful in intelligence tests. Most intelligence tests test a very limited range of skills and abilities such as verbal reasoning, but Gardner argues that people have a much broader range of abilities than that. He initially listed seven but has now extended the list to nine. These are set out in Table 3.2 (page 29).

Traditional teaching emphasises the mathematical-logical and the linguistic. In your design of learners' experiences, you need to take account of the fact that your learners will have greater or lesser abilities in all these areas. Otherwise you are permanently disadvantaging those learners whose strengths are neither mathematical-logical nor linguistic.

A good way to consider the whole range is to draw up a planning sheet for each topic. Put the topic title in the middle, then draw a box for each intelligence. In each box put a strategy you could use to suit a learner with that sort of intelligence. Figure 3.4 is an example I have completed for the use of e-learning in a communication key skills course.

Individual learning styles

The focus of many of the developments in our understanding of learning is the individual student's learning style. Teachers have long known that all learners are different; the best way for any one learner to learn will not be the same as the best way for another learner. What we have needed is a way of capturing and summarising those differences.

Intelligence	Abilities
linguistic	able to work with words; ease with reading and writing
visual-spatial	able to see things in pictures; to relate to where things are; to navigate; to see patterns
logical mathematical	able to work things through logically; to follow sequences; to calculate
inter-personal	able to work effectively with other people; to be aware of their emotional states and respond appropriately
intra-personal	very aware of own self; able to reflect; to evaluate own position; to plan
musical-rhythmic	able to make music; to respond to aural patterns
bodily-kinaesthetic	able to control and use your body physically; to move skilfully; to know where your fingertips are
spiritual	aware of spiritual values; sensitivity to those things which make us human
environmental	very aware of the physical world; able to identify and respond to changes in the environment

Table 3.2 Multiple intelligence

One straightforward classification, presented in Table 3.3, is to divide people into three categories according to how they most readily deal with the world – by visual, auditory or kinaesthetic means. This is often referred to as the VAK model.

Children have a preference for the kinaesthetic. By the time we reach adulthood, the visual is generally the strongest. However, most people have a combination of all three.

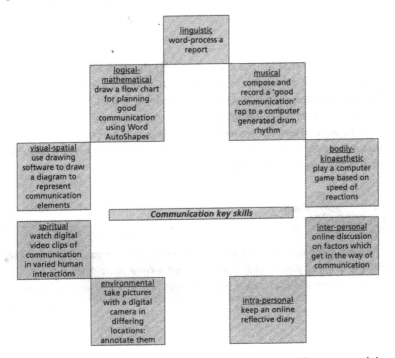

Figure 3.4 A planning grid based on the multiple intelligence model

Preferred representation	Learning through	Ways of learning
visual	seeing	Uses diagrams, pictures and maps. Watching demonstrations and videos. Visualising
auditory	hearing	Likes discussions, explanations, and instructions. Talking to oneself
kinaesthetic	physical activities	Uses touching, moving, experiencing. Remembered emotions and movements

Table 3.3 Preferred learning styles

Michael Grinder, neuro-linguistic programming (NLP) proponent, estimates that, out of a group of 30 students, typically 22 have enough VAK abilities to cope regardless of how a lesson is presented. Two or three students have difficulty learning regardless of presenting style, due to factors outside the classroom. The other students have a very heavy preference for one learning style.

PRACTICAL TASK PRACTICAL TASK PRACTICAL TASK PRACTICAL TASK PRACTICAL TASK

For each of the visual, auditory and kinaesthetic learning styles, identify teaching and learning strategies that you could use in face-to-face sessions and in e-learning. Table 3.4 (page 31) has some suggestions to start you thinking.

We are certainly getting much better at identifying each learner's individual characteristics through diagnostic tests. Many of these can be conducted by computer and the internet gives access to a whole plethora. Probably the best known British example is the Honey and Mumford Learning Styles questionnaire, available, for a small fee, on the Peter Honey website. This analyses learners in relation to the stages of the Kolb experiential learning cycle – see the earlier part of this chapter. It classifies learners as Activists, Reflectors, Theorists and Pragmatists. On the FERL website, you can read about how West Kent College assessed the learning styles of all their first-year learners using Studyscan software.

Alternatively, there are plenty of websites with questionnaires that will analyse your learning style, and those of your students, for nothing. There is also no guarantee as to how perceptive and reliable the questionnaires are. Just like anything you find on the internet, use your judgement. Always ask yourself 'Who says so and how do they know?' All the sites here come from educational institutions, which means that they are of course absolutely, absolutely totally reliable. Possibly.

North Carolina State University www2.ncsu.edu/unity/lockers/users/f/felder/public/ILSdir/ilsweb.html

James Cook University www.jcu.edu.au/studying/services/studyskillslearningst/download and run the programme brain.exe

Chaminade College Preparatory School www.chaminade.org/inspire/learnstl.htm

Honolulu Community College www.hcc.hawaii.edu/intranet/committees/FacDevCom/guidebk/teachtip/vark.htm

Preferred representation	Face-to-face learning strategies	E-learning strategies
visual	• learning maps • draw/write on a white board/ flipchart • use a highlighter • sit quietly and visualise	• onscreen diagrams • use a highlighter in your word processor
auditory	• read out loud • oral summarising and explaining • record audio tapes	• use computer programs with sound • record audio clips
kinaesthetic	• walk about while learning • sort cards • write explanations • complete checklists	• use the mouse to carry out a task • watch video clips and complete – by hand – an observation checklist

Table 3.4 Learning styles and e-learning

Once you have diagnosed your learning style, the question is then, 'So what?' What we cannot yet do is fine-tune learning activities so that each is specific to the individual learner – a visual learner can work more visually and a kinaesthetic learner can work more physically. In one view of the future, this is what the power of the computer will enable us to do. I have my doubts – learning is a social activity and I am concerned that individualisation could mean isolation.

Teaching tip

In the short term, you can do the following:

• Ensure that in planning you include something for everybody. Follow an activity where the learner has to sort on-screen boxes, each containing one stage in a process, into the appropriate order, with an activity requiring learners to compose a rap about a principle to a drum and bass accompaniment In other words, an activity for the logical/mathematical learner is followed by one for the musical rhythmic person.

• Give your learners choices, so they can select the ways of learning they like best. For example, where at one time you might have set an essay to write, now you could encourage them to choose alternatives such as an audio recording, a PowerPoint presentation or a mind map – or the verbal learner could still write the essay. It helps too if you raise your learners' awareness of how they learn.

REFLECTIVE TASK
REFLECTIVE TASK

Look back at the ideas about effective learning in this chapter. Write a paragraph or so in your diary or on your blog about the principles your teaching is based on and how you might adapt them to e-learning.

Visual overview

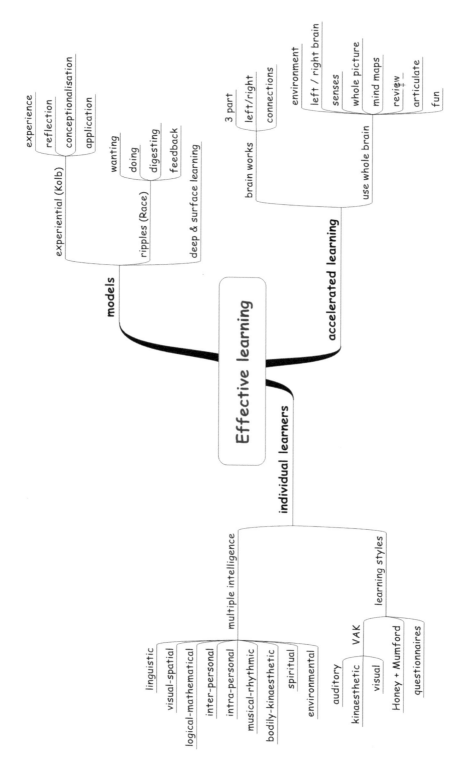

Many teachers adopt a pragmatic approach. If a teaching strategy works we will use it. However, teaching is more effective when it is based on understanding. This chapter has set out some models that should inform that understanding.

In the next chapter we will look at the forms that e-learning can take and explore some of the barriers that get in the way of its successful use.

REFERENCES AND FURTHER READING REFERENCES AND FURTHER READING

Ashcroft, K. and Foreman-Peck, L. (1994) *Managing teaching and learning in further and higher education*. London: Falmer Press.

Ellington, H., Percival, F. and Race, P. (1993) *A handbook of educational technology*. London: Kogan Page.

Hattie, J. (1999) *Influences on student learning*. Available online at www.education.auckland.ac.nz/voa/education/staff/j.hattie/papers/influences.cfm (accessed 23 September 2007).

Kolb, D.A. (1984) *Experiential learning – experience as a source of learning and development*. Englewood Cliffs: Prentice Hall.

Rose, C. and Nicholl, M. J. (1997) *Accelerated learning for the twenty-first century*. London: Piatkus.

Smith, A. (1996) *Accelerated learning*. Stafford: Network Press.

Websites

web.uvic.ca/hrd/halfbaked/ Hot Potatoes assessment software, free of charge for non-profit educational users who make their pages available on the web. The FERL website offers the facility to post your quizzes on the web at ferl.qia.org.uk

www.phil-race.net/ Phil Race's personal website.

www.questionmark.com/uk/home.htm Question Mark commercial assessment software.

www.peterhoney.com/ The Honey and Mumford Learning Styles questionnaire.

ferl.qia.org.uk has many relevant resources.

http://sourceforge.net/projects/freemind You can download the free open source mindmapping software here.

4
The role of e-learning

This chapter will help you to:

- **survey the different forms that e-learning can take;**
- **describe different roles that e-learning can fill;**
- **take account of some of the limitations of e-learning.**

LLUK Standards relevant to this chapter include:
BP3.1, CK3.5, CP3.5, DP1.2, EK1.2, EP1.2.

The range of e-learning

In Chapter 2 there are four examples of e-learning in action which illustrate very different situations. They range from elements of e-learning added into traditional face-to-face classes right the way through to the whole course being taught online with no tutor/learner or learner/learner face-to-face contact, with many variations in between.

Scribbens and Powell (2003) set this out as a fan with seven segments, shown in Figure 4.1. Six of the segments represent the progression from using e-learning as a traditional learning tool to anytime-anywhere learning. The seventh, 'Supporting learning', represents activities outside of the scheduled learning programme but which complement the formal learning programme, such as internet research.

I've used the word 'progression' but it does not mean that everything is moving towards remote learning or that remote learning is better than the other segments. What is progressing is learner autonomy, the opportunity for learners to make their own decisions about their learning programme.

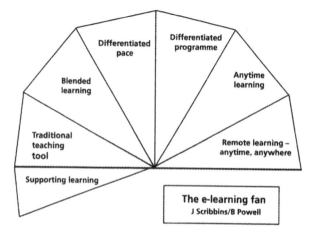

Figure 4.1 The e-learning fan

Table 4.1 takes a closer look at the different segments of the e-learning fan. It describes what is meant by each segment, sets out the role that e-learning plays, gives an example and identifies the decisions that the learner makes.

Pattern of e-learning	Description	Possible e-learning role	Examples	Learner decision making
traditional teaching tool	e-learning enabling traditional teaching to work better	• to enhance delivery, like an improved visual aid • showing a video clip	• PowerPoint presentations	Tutor makes the decisions and may offer choices
blended learning	a planned mixture of traditional learning and e-learning across a whole programme	• to complement traditional learning	• internet research in preparation for face-to-face sessions	More real choices offered to the learner
differentiated place	learners can work at their own speed	• tracking learner progress • delivering material and activities • means of tutor support	• working through a self-study tutorial learning how to use a spreadsheet	Am I ready to move on to the next bit? Do it again?
differentiated programme	an agreed individualised programme for each learner	• initial assessments • tracking learner progress • delivering material and activities	• means of tutor support • various routes through a programme of material, including remedial sections and sections of extension work	What are my needs?
anytime learning	accessing the learning programme at any time the college (or wherever the facility available) is open	• tracking learner progress • delivering material and activities • means of tutor support	• accessing materials held on an intranet or shared network drive	When shall I do it?
remote learning	anytime – anywhere learning from remote locations	• tracking learner progress • delivery of material • and activities • online peer and tutor support	• courses delivered entirely online	When and where shall I do it?
supporting learning	activities to complement the main learning programme	• communication tool • access to information	• online discussions • online research	What support do I need?

Table 4.1 The segments of the e-learning fan

Thus e-learning can take many different forms. As we develop our use of e-learning it certainly does not mean that all learning will be done online without anyone having to put a foot outside his or her front door. For most people, learning is a social activity and physically meeting and working with other learners is one of the major attractions. Meeting online is a substitute, albeit an inferior one. A webcam, a small camera that captures pictures to send over the internet, can help.

In some cases, anytime-anywhere learning is by far the most appropriate. For delivering a course on highway repair to a limited number of road maintenance engineers who are scattered right the way across the country and very busy in full-time employment, a totally online course is ideal. Course members can study when and where they want; all they need is access to the internet. The alternatives would be paper-based distance learning, which experience shows would have a high drop-out rate, or short intensive courses which would involve the disruption of having to stay away from home. It is also easier for the course provider because there are only a limited number of people with the skills and experience necessary to tutor such a course. The flexibility of tutoring the course online from home and at convenient times increases the availability of tutors. There is clearly a tutor training need: but there is a training need for face-to-face teachers as well.

Many of us are most likely to be concerned with blended learning – a planned mixture of e-learning and traditional teaching. A healthy way to see e-learning is to regard it as another tool, albeit a powerful one, in the toolkit for delivering learning. It then becomes a question of selecting the appropriate tool for a particular aspect of the teaching/learning job. Sometimes that tool is an e-learning tool and sometimes not.

So what does blended learning look like? Here are two examples. They are taken from a typical further education college.

Example 1

In a group learning advanced Italian, course members are required to prepare a short talk to be delivered in a class session on a topic currently in the news. They research it by visiting the websites of Italian newspapers. After the class they work in small groups to prepare a single page – in Italian – about the issue to go onto a course website. The tutor has also established a link with a group learning English in a college in Milan. Course members have e-mail pen friends in the Italian college, and the two institutions are working towards a video conference that will be held later in the term.

Example 2

In an HNC computing module on web page design, course members have to complete a simulated project where they design a website for a customer. It is organised in a way that includes a mixture of e-learning – internet research, use of project management software, e-mailed confirmation of project outputs – with traditional aspects – written brief, group work to explore possible difficulties in completing the project, role-play negotiation with a client and write up of final evaluation.

Both of these examples could have been run without any e-learning at all and both of them could have been entirely e-learning. In fact they blend together a mixture of e-learning and traditional learning and the student experience is enriched as a result. In the language example, there is no viable alternative to accessing that day's news in the target language on websites. Printed foreign newspapers are expensive and take days to arrive. The international exchange of e-mails is much quicker – and therefore much more motivating – than conventional post. In the computing example, learners gain experience of using commercial software that will stand them in good stead when they apply for jobs, and the time that is available for face-to-face contact is used for high-payoff activities such as the role play. Successful blended learning is about balance and using each strategy appropriately.

PRACTICAL TASK PRACTICAL TASK PRACTICAL TASK PRACTICAL TASK PRACTICAL TASK

For a course that you teach or could teach, decide what blend of e-learning and traditional learning you would use. Make a note of a reason for each of your decisions.

The potential roles of e-learning

The LLUK Professional Standards for Teachers, Tutors and Trainers in the Lifelong Learning Sector are a map of the territory within which further education teachers operate. The Standards identify six domains within which teachers work. Which of them can ILT play a role in? It is not difficult to identify examples. In Table 4.2 I've set out the six domains and made some suggestions for the use of ILT. What other examples can you think of?

Domain	e-learning/ILT example
A – Professional Values and Practice	<ul><li>keeping a reflective diary on a blog</li><li>contributing to an online discussion group about practical teaching issues</li><li>e-mail relationship with a mentor</li></ul>
B – Learning and Teaching	<ul><li>interactive worksheets</li><li>texting work schedule by mobile phone to learners who miss a session</li><li>tracking what learners have done and what they have achieved</li></ul>
C – Specialist Learning and Teaching	<ul><li>learners contributing to a wiki on an aspect of your subject area subject</li><li>specific software, e.g. virtual dissection in biology</li><li>video-conference with a subject expert</li></ul>
D – Planning for Learning	<ul><li>designing blended learning programmes</li><li>preparing interactive teaching materials</li><li>planning use of multimedia material</li></ul>
E – Assessment for Learning	<ul><li>computer-marked formative assessments to give learners feedback on their progress</li><li>transcript of contribution to online discussion as evidence in candidate portfolio</li><li>online diagnostic tests</li></ul>
F – Access and Progression	<ul><li>developing an e-portfolio</li><li>technology to assist learners with particular needs such as screen readers</li><li>course information published on website</li></ul>

Table 4.2 Potential roles of ILT

This is saying something very simple, but that nonetheless needs saying. E-learning potentially has a role to play in all the key areas of teaching and supporting learning. All you have to do is select the right tool from the toolkit.

Why not e-learning?

So are there any reasons for not choosing an e-learning tool from the toolkit when one is available? Petty, well known in further education for his work on raising achievement, identifies four things to think about when choosing appropriate teaching methods (Petty 2004). The factors are:

- **what teaching methods are available;**
- **the strengths and weaknesses of the methods;**
- **the purpose of each method;**
- **how to use each method.**

Exactly the same applies whether you are dealing with traditional methods or e-learning. Encouragingly, there is never one best method to use. The art of teaching is to assess the needs and options for each situation and decide accordingly. Ten teachers could choose ten different ways of doing it, and each one be right. A variety helps, partly because it adds interest for the learners and partly because different methods will suit different learners.

We will look at specific e-learning tools in later chapters, but for now we will consider two issues that relate to e-learning as an overall strategy, starting with the crucial question of accessibility. The second issue is technical reliability.

Accessibility

Accessibility is concerned with minimising barriers that prevent learners taking a full part in the learning process. The barriers may prevent learners getting onto a course in the first place. These include the cost of course fees, childcare difficulties and lack of formal qualifications. Once on a course there are other barriers such as dyslexia, the cost of books and physical conditions such as poor eyesight. Inclusion involves finding ways to integrate learners with particular needs into mainstream provision.

We have already seen that, by minimising difficulties of time and place, e-learning can greatly increase accessibility of courses. However, e-learning does require access to the kit. The surveys carried out by BECTA of the number of computers per student in FE colleges show that the target of one computer to five students had been met by 2002. However, that is not the same thing as saying that all students can access a computer when they need one. Many of the computers are in teaching rooms used for timetabled classes so that students can only access them during formal taught sessions. This is very different to the situation where sufficient computers are open access, perhaps on a bookable basis, with tutor support.

Further issues arise over home access to a computer. The 2005–06 Expenditure and Food Survey (Office of National Statistics, 2006) shows that 65 per cent of households have a computer – two in three. Most of these are able to access the internet – 55 per cent of households have access to the internet. Equal opportunities issues arise. It is much more difficult for people living in households without a computer to access online and blended learning courses, and the survey shows that one in three households do not have a computer. Furthermore, among households in the highest income group, 95 per cent had a home computer and 93 per cent an internet connection, compared with 29 and 17 per cent of households in the lowest income group.

There are regional variations too. The Expenditure and Food Survey shows that the United Kingdom region with the best access has significantly higher proportions of homes with a computer than the worst region. London has 68 per cent of households with a computer and 58 per cent with internet access; Northern Ireland has 52 per cent of households with a computer and 41 per cent with internet access. Like many regional statistics, it is the peripheral regions that fare worst: the further you get from London and the south east, the lower the proportion of households with a computer. This is another manifestation of the fact that higher income households are much more likely to have a computer at home.

This means that many of your students will not have home access to a computer. It will obviously vary from course to course. For my teacher training courses, informal surveys show that two-thirds of course members have a computer at home. For other courses the proportion will be much lower. I wondered for a while whether I should hold back from setting out-of-class tasks that needed a computer because it would disadvantage those learners without a computer at home. Similarly, should I insist that assignments must be word-processed? On talking this through with the course members, they pointed out that every course member does have access to free computer facilities in the college learning centre and also in their local libraries. The parallel was also drawn with access to books. Some households – again, usually those with higher income levels – will have more books for learners to draw on. Would I not recommend reading because not everyone could afford to buy a book?

Teaching tip

Ask your learners about their access to computers to carry out tasks you set and, in the light of what you hear, ensure you give sufficient time for tasks to be completed for those who have to wait for access. Make sure you make clear what computer facilities are available within your organisation.

Computers can also help with on-course accessibility. Sometimes this needs particular pieces of kit – adaptive technology. For example, users might find a tracker ball easier than a mouse. Voice-recognition and screen reading software can be very helpful for learners who cannot see well or who have poor reading and writing skills. Very often accessibility simply means setting up the computer in the most appropriate way. For example, some learners need text of a big enough size or may find a particular colour combination more straightforward to read. The changes are relatively easy to make once you know how and once you are sufficiently informed to realise what might help. Since Windows 95, Windows operating systems have included Accessibility choices – look them up using Help from the Start menu.

There is a growing recognition that if things were designed in the first place so that the majority of people could use them, there would be much less need for specialist equipment. The principle is called Universal Design and it benefits everyone, not only disabled people. It is no more difficult or costly to design material with good readability in the first place.

Teaching tip

When you prepare handouts and worksheets, if you choose a font without serifs such as Arial, many people with dyslexia find it easier to read than a font with serifs. Fonts without serifs are cleaner and the shape of each letter is simpler because there are no extra bits sticking out.

This is Arial, a font without serifs.

This is Times New Roman, a font with serifs.

If you design materials for online learning – or select such materials – Universal Design should be fundamental. To help you, there are a number of free tools on the internet that will check how accessible your web pages are; one example is on the TechDis website.

JISC funds its TechDis service to work with all staff in educational institutions to provide contextualised help and advice on all aspects of technology and disabilities. It has a database of several thousand examples of assistive technology and all users of e-learning should read its booklet (Phipps, Sutherland and Searle, 2002). A further source of help and advice is the AbilityNet charity. This is a group who works to find ways of adapting computers to meet learner needs.

Technical ability

ICT kit is fine when it all works – but it is not always like that. It can refuse to do what you want it to do. It can stop working half-way through. It can do the completely unexpected and refuse to go back to familiar territory. It has a mind of its own. What can you do?

- **Prepare carefully; try it out on your own or with a colleague so you are comfortable with what you want to do.**
- **Draw on your learners' knowledge. Don't feel threatened if your learners know more than you – it is a resource: use it. Perhaps you could make learners responsible for the kit. And don't underestimate the power of you, the teacher, being prepared to share what you cannot do with your learners. Don't you want them to tell you what they cannot do, or would you rather they covered that up?**
- **Know where to get help – and use it. Have you heard people complain that the kit isn't working as they would like yet, when you ask, they have not reported it to anyone?**
- **Learn very basic maintenance. The staff on the ICT helpdesk in my former college say that over a third of help requests they get about kit not working are resolved by asking the caller to check that all cables are firmly connected and all the kit is switched on.**

Imagine that you are going to drive to a place you have never been to before that is far away. You would prepare for the journey by looking up the way on the map beforehand and you would take the map with you. You would do a basic maintenance checks for petrol and (perhaps) tyres, oil and water. If the car breaks down you are unlikely to dismantle it by the roadside; you will call for help from someone who knows. It is exactly the same with ICT kit. You might be discouraged from making the trip if you felt your car was not reliable, but generally you make the trip because the car serves its purpose: it is a means to an end. The computer in teaching and learning is exactly the same.

But don't forget that face-to-face teaching can breakdown as well. The overhead projector bulb will blow or the OHP not be there; material you have based the whole session around can be greeted with cries of 'We've done this before'. Would you find it too sickly if I suggested that something going wrong might present an opportunity? You might discuss with your learners why you were using the kit in the first place, so enabling them to become more aware of the learning process and giving them the chance to choose alternatives for themselves. I work in a college that has a very high reliance on e-mail for communication. From time to time it inevitably breaks down. And I re-learn the pleasure of going and talking to my colleagues.

You need to think about what your learners will experience from the technology too. What do you know about the machines that your learners will be using for their e-learning? This is partly a question of what their machines are capable of doing and what they are actually set up to do. Over time, computers are becoming more powerful and there is a big difference between what the newest computers will do and what the average computer will do. The temptation is for material to use the full potential of the new machines with video, graphics and sound but this may not run happily when accessed from less powerful machines many students may have. Similarly, it can be intimidating if, the first time a learner accesses their online course from home, a dialogue box appears on the screen asking if they want to install whatever extra bit of software (plug in) is needed to see all the animations. And I know of more than one college where the vast majority of student computers have sound cards, but are not set up to play sound, and there are not enough headphones for students to use anyway.

REFLECTIVE TASK
REFLECTIVE TASK

Look back at the ideas you have met in this chapter about the roles for e-learning and some of the difficulties in implementing them. Write a paragraph or so in your diary or on your blog about how the ideas relate to the learners you teach or could teach.

IGNPOST ▶ In this chapter we have viewed e-learning as one part of the teacher's toolkit which, like all the other tools, has its own uses. We have also looked at two particular issues, access to kit and technical issues.

In the next chapter we will look at the range of e-learning tools that are available – although maybe not all of them to you or me – and how you can use them.

Visual overview

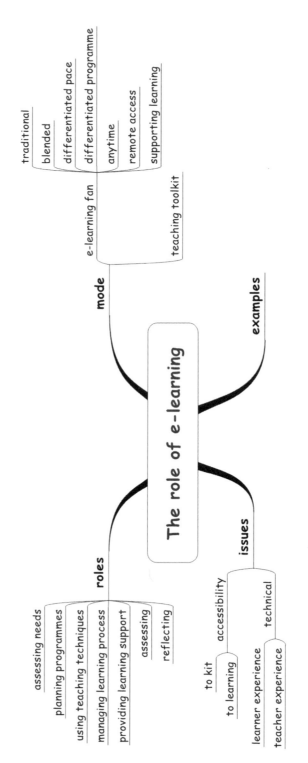

REFERENCES AND FURTHER READING REFERENCES AND FURTHER READING

Office of National Statistics (2007) *Family Spending 2005–06 – A report on the Expenditure and Food Survey*. London, Office of National Statistics available online at www.statistics.gov.uk/ (accessed 7 June 2007).

Petty, G. (2004) *Teaching today* (3rd edition revised). Cheltenham: Nelson Thornes.

Phipps, L., Sutherland, A. and Searle, J. (eds) (2002) *Access all areas: disability, technology and learning*. York: TechDis/JISC/Association for Learning Technology. Downloadable from the TechDis website www.techdis.ac.uk (accessed 7 June 2007).

Scribbins, J. and Powell, B. (2003) *Managing inspection and ILT*. Downloadable from the ferl section of the Excellence Gateway website http://ferl.qia.org.uk (accessed 7 June 2007). Enter the title in the site search engine.

Websites

www.abilitynet.co.uk For help in adapting computers to learner needs.

www.lluk.org The website of Lifelong Learning UK, source of the professional standards in the sector.

www.statistics.gov.uk/ The government statistics site contains everything you could want to know and much more besides. Enter Family Spending in the search box.

www.techdis.ac.uk/ TechDis is a JISC service aimed at increasing access to teaching and learning for those with learning difficulties and/or disabilities. Brilliant.

5
The tools and how to use them

This chapter will help you to:

- **describe the diversity of e-learning tools available;**
- **select appropriate e-learning tools;**
- **view ICT tools as e-learning tools;**
- **incorporate appropriate strategies into your teaching/training.**

The LLUK Standards relevant to this chapter include:
BP3.1, BP5.1, CK3.5, CP3.5, DP1.2, EK1.2, EP1.2.

The emphasis in this chapter is on practical ideas. As you work through it, make a note of examples you could apply to your own teaching and learning. You may not have access to all the tools identified in the first part of the chapter, but most of the ideas require basic facilities and a bit of imagination. There is a big difference between what e-learning tools might do and what we as teachers get them to do.

Table 5.1 identifies some of the tools that you might find available for e-learning. We cannot look at all the possible tools, neither can we go into technical detail. What I will do is to set out what the main characteristics of the tools are.

PRACTICAL TASK PRACTICAL TASK PRACTICAL TASK PRACTICAL TASK PRACTICAL TASK

As you work through the range of tools, find out which are available to you. Classify them into tools you use currently and ones that you would want to use.

We will start with complete systems.

Virtual learning environments and managed learning environments

The JISC managed learning environment (MLE) steering group defines a virtual learning environment (VLE) as the part of a college's systems 'in which learners and tutors participate in on-line interactions of various kinds, including on-line learning' (accessed online). Exactly – but what does it mean? In practice it means that the VLE is a piece of software that:

Category	Tool	Characteristic
integrated system	managed learning environment	integrated systems and processes that contribute to learning and management of learning
	virtual learning environment	integrated system for delivering and supporting learning
communication	internet link	access to the world wide web: e-mail; college website(s)
	intranet	website only accessible from inside the college
	network shared drives	computers in the college linked together, with shared facilities such as printers and file storage
software	generic, e.g. word processing	not subject specific nor with learning as its prime purpose
	specific, e.g. typing tuition program	specifically designed as a learning tool; subject specific
hardware	computers	desktop; laptop; tablet, personal digital assistant (PDA)
	computer peripherals	scanner, printer; digital camera, digital camcorder
	personal equipment	mobile phone, MP3 player
	classroom equipment	interactive whiteboard; data projector; visualiser

Table 5.1 Some tools for e-learning

- **enables the learner to communicate with other learners and with tutors;**
- **lets the learner access their curriculum in small chunks of learning, each of which can be assessed and tracked;**
- **lets the tutor monitor what the learner does and what the learner achieves;**
- **supports online learning by giving access to resources and guidance.**

Figure 5.1 shows a virtual learning environment called the Virtual Campus, which I used to deliver the Certificate in the Educational Use of the Internet. Course members, who can access the course from anywhere that they can access the internet, are each given their own log-in protected by a password. When they log in, what they see is personalised to them: it uses their name, it links to previous times they have logged in and they can bookmark the place where they left off working last time. The course material, which includes information, activities and assessments, is set out on the menu on the left-hand side of the screen. The activities often link the learner to other course members, for example asking them to share their reaction to a particular piece of reading. There are frequent assessment tasks, which are automatically marked, and feedback is given to the learners.

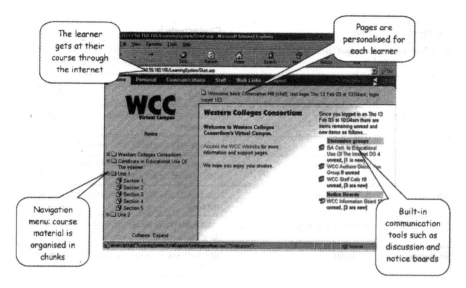

Figure 5.1 The Virtual Campus virtual learning environment

Learners work at their own rate, and in the order that they like, although they are given a suggested timetable so they have something to compare their progress with. There are built-in study tools to help the learner, for example a calendar and progress record. As tutor I can check the progress of every learner, to see who has logged on, when they logged on, what pages they visited and the results of their assessments.

In practice I logged on most days in order to answer learners' queries. It would be much less effective if learners had to wait days before getting a response. If a course member is quiet for a while or is getting behind with the work, I contact them to give them a bit of encouragement. Good practice is exactly the same as in face-to-face tutoring but the context is different.

FERL has a specific Focus Area on Virtual Learning Environments which is well worth a visit. There are lots of VLEs to choose from; the Edutools website has recent user reviews of 24 different VLEs. In the next chapter we will explore more about VLEs and how you can use them with your learners.

Further education used to use the term 'managed learning environment' instead of virtual learning environment: VLE was a higher education term. It did not take long, however, before it was pointed out that an FE college is itself a learning environment where lots of things are managed, including students, resources and rooms. A VLE does not operate in isolation. A college will have electronic and paper records for student enrolments, exam entry and registers. The term managed learning environment is now used for 'the whole range of information systems and processes of a college (including its VLE if it has one) that contribute directly or indirectly to learning and the management of that learning'. The definition comes once again from the JISC MLE Steering Group.

The relationship between the VLE and the MLE is illustrated in Figure 5.2 (page 47). It shows the different components making up the managed learning environment surrounding the six elements which make up the virtual learning environment.

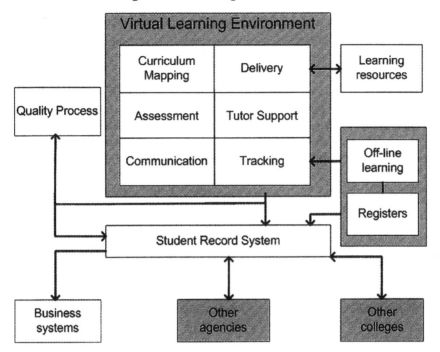

Figure 5.2 The managed learning environment

The arrows indicate some of the links between the different components. The ideal is that information can pass smoothly and quickly between the different components of a college's MLE. For example:

- **when a student enrols in the college on a particular course, a log-in is automatically created in the VLE, giving the student access to just the online material they need;**
- **the time students spend using the VLE is fed to the register system;**
- **results of student assessments in the VLE would be passed back to the student record system.**

Data also needs to be transferred outside of the college, in particular to the Learning and Skills Council, which provides much of the funding for post-16 education and training.

In the average college, the different components of the MLE will often be made by different firms and installed at different times. In practice, it is not always easy to move data between them. For information to move painlessly, there must be clear rules that everyone follows. MLEs and VLEs are in the process of adopting a set of standards called IMS. Any future purchases must be standards compliant.

Websites

As part of the LSC investment, all colleges have a high-speed (now usually at least 10 megabit) link to the internet through the JANET system. The same facility has been offered to Adult and Community Learning managing agents; to date about half of them have taken it up. Access to the internet gives a very valuable set of tools, including the college website, the world wide web and e-mail.

Its website is the public electronic face of a learning provider and it:

- **gives information about courses on offer;**
- **gives information about the organisation;**
- **is a marketing tool;**
- **gives access from other locations to internal services, for example the VLE or library catalogue.**

The effectiveness of a website depends on its design and its content. Content means that what the user wants to find is there; design means they can find it. Content should be relevant and up to date. Design is a mixture of structure and appearance.

- **Good structure, along with an effective menu and navigation system, means that it is easy to get to the information the user needs. How patient are you when you visit a website? Conventional wisdom has it that you should be able to find what you want in a maximum of three clicks from the home page.**
- **Appearance is much more than how attractive a page looks, although clearly that helps.**
  - **How readable is the website? Is it written for *Guardian* readers or for *Sun* readers?**
  - **Does it recognise the fact that most of us have a visual preference, although graphics slow down the speed with which a web page loads?**
  - **Does it adopt Universal Design? Universal Design is 'the design of products and environments that can be used and experienced by people of all ages and abilities, to the greatest extent possible, without adaptation' (Phipps, Sutherland and Searle, 2002).**
  - **Does it have a text-only version for those people with a slow internet connection?**

Visit the RNIB website to have a look at their campaign for good web design.

Good design also affects speed. Various figures are quoted for how long someone will wait for a page to load: 7 seconds is my rule of thumb. A well-designed page will load much quicker.

Teaching tip

Use your college website to recruit to your courses. Find out how you can put material on it. How can you make a special feature of the things you want to highlight – a new course, 100 per cent achievement rates or a new facility you will be using? Ask a friend to visit the website and find details of your courses. How easy is it?

Intranet

An intranet is a website that is visible only from within an organisation. In a college, the intranet might be used simply to present information for students and staff about all the services available, as a sort of electronic handbook. If you want to find out about the college counselling service or when the canteen is open, up-to-date detail should be on the intranet. But intranets can do much more than this. Have a look at the intranet case studies on the FERL website, including that of North Tyneside College. In this college, the intranet is used primarily as a curriculum delivery tool. Tutors – and often students – put learning materials on the intranet. Students access these materials either in directed learning sessions or in their own time.

Materials have to be prepared to go onto the intranet. Usually this means they are web pages; sometimes they are in other forms, for example Acrobat (pdf) files. Either tutors need training so they can do this or specialist staff have to be employed. But the bigger change is in the independence of the learner. Tutors need to know how to incorporate intranet resources into their teaching programmes so that learning is maximised.

Network shared drives

If the computers in an organisation are linked together they form a network. On a network you will also find facilities such as printers and scanners. There will also be one or more computers which run the network; these are normally called servers. The computers on a network are usually linked by physical cables but may be linked wirelessly. Wireless networks give the user more flexibility, but often run more slowly than systems connected by wire. Networks have a number of advantages.

- **They allow peripherals such as printers to be shared between users, giving better value for money.**
- **They give access to a greater range of peripherals; all the peripherals attached to the network can be accessed from any computer.**
- **Networks are managed, which means that someone does much of the housekeeping for the individual user, especially keeping backups. The management also includes security, controlling who can access what.**
- **A user can access their own work from any computer on the network.**

One of the facilities a network will provide for each of its registered users is space to store files. Different users will have different areas to store their files in. There will be areas for students and tutors to store their own work, areas for tutors to store files that other tutors can access and areas for tutors to make files available to their students. An alternative to providing course material on an intranet is to make material available on drives that can be accessed by particular groups of students. These are called the student shared drives. Users can be given different rights for the different storage areas. For example, files in the area where tutors make files available to students will usually be read-only: students can open the files to read them and use them, but cannot save them.

Any sort of file can be stored on the shared drive, not only web pages.This means that there is less of a training need for tutors. However, it does require that tutors and students are happy with basic file housekeeping. In a Windows system, they must be comfortable with Windows Explorer or My Computer. My own experience is that many tutors are not as comfortable with this as they should be. In a way it is inevitable. It is only when you cannot find yet another file that you think you ought to do something about it.

Teaching tip

Be very systematic in the way you store your files. Use long names for your files that make sense to you now and will make sense in six months' time. Create lots of folders to keep your files in. Create folders in your folders. Delete files you don't want any more. If you don't know how to create folders, find out now! One way of finding out is to take the first part of the European Computer Driving Licence.

Putting material on an intranet or shared drives system opens up all sorts of possible strategies for teaching, which we will explore later.

Software

Much of the software that you will use in e-learning was not originally designed to be a learning tool. It was probably designed to be an office efficiency tool and only finds itself accidentally being used in an educational context. Nonetheless, it is immensely valuable; it is hard to think of managing without a word processor. Other software in learning providers is specifically designed for educational purposes, from the software that stores student records, to the systems used for managing the library catalogue and programs designed for particular learning activities and topics.

Software is expensive and there is a temptation to copy it or 'borrow' disks from work and install it at home. The advice is simple: don't do it. It is theft. There are, however, a number of things you can do to reduce the cost of software both for your organisation and for yourself as an individual.

- Ask about educational prices. For example, many of the most popular Microsoft products such as Office are available at substantially reduced prices to teachers and registered students.
- Use the CHEST system. CHEST is an organisation that negotiates agreements and offers for use by the educational community, generally on a site licence basis. Visit the CHEST website to see the directory of what is available.
- Co-ordinate orders. The price per copy is often lower if you order several copies, so identify who else might want to buy.
- Read licence agreements. Some licence agreements let teachers install a copy on their home computer of programs they use extensively at work.

Hardware – all the bits and pieces of kit

PRACTICAL TASK PRACTICAL TASK PRACTICAL TASK PRACTICAL TASK PRACTICAL TASK

Take a blank piece of paper. Imagine that someone with more money than sense has asked you to design a learning environment equipped with all the e-learning tools that you could usefully use. Sketch out a diagram of what you would like. Amend your diagram as you read through the material that follows.

My ideal teaching room has plenty of space so that learners can move around; flexible, comfortable furniture, which can be re-organised to suit a variety of uses; efficient and controllable lighting, ventilation and heating so that learners are comfortable; copious display facilities. It would be well decorated and have resilient but attractive carpets. None of this is specifically related to e-learning, and that is the way it should be. First and foremost I want to create an environment for learning, and the kit comes afterwards. Nonetheless, the explosion in recent years of different bits of kit opens up lots of possibilities for creative teaching and learning.

In Table 5.2 I set out some of the bits of kit I would like.

	Purpose	Find out about	Example of use
scanner	capture visual material into digital form so it can be manipulated and used on computer	• resolution • can it handle transparencies and negatives as well as paper?	• capture graphics to include in worksheets
digital camera	capture still images	• resolution • memory • how pictures are transferred to computer	• learners create display about topics under study
data projector	project computer screen onto wall projector	• brightness • ceiling mounting • operation by remote control	• use for learner presentations
interactive whiteboard	sensitive whiteboard with built-in projector software	• durability • software that comes with it	• operate software by touching the whiteboard
colour printer	printing on paper and other media	• cost of refills	• learners prepare overhead transparencies
web cam	small camera feeding directly into computer	• how often picture updated • quality	• video conference with other educational institution, including abroad
visualiser	updated version of the overhead projector which works using a digital camera rather than mirrors; image fed into computer from where it can be projected	• what is needed to project the image	• projecting finished work, maps, coloured graphics, 3D objects

Table 5.2 Wish list of e-learning kit

What is not included in the table is the computer itself. Obviously, there are different sorts of computers, each with different merits. A number of colleges have made the decision to equip members of teaching staff with laptop computers. It is certainly an attraction to staff to find that their college values them sufficiently to give them the proper tools to do the job. Historically, many lecturers have decided to buy their own computer for home use. It's a bit like Marks and Spencer asking cashiers to buy their own tills.

In some cases the laptops are able to connect to the college network wirelessly. Wireless laptop computing has the potential to totally transform the teacher's working life. Here is a description of what the lecturer's working days might be like, given that kit.

Two days in the life of a mobile lecturer

DAY 1

Take wireless laptop to college. Find an empty hotdesk to use. Log into college network to check e-mail – no cables to connect.

Go to first class. Connect laptop to projector wirelessly to show presentations the students have prepared as the basis of class discussions. Students use remote mouse during presentation.

In later economics class, one group of students uses the laptop (again wireless connection) to connect to Government Statistical Office website so they can find latest employment figures.

Over lunchtime use laptop to write reference. Save it (wireless) to the college network. Print it out.

For afternoon class, again link laptop to projector to use mind-mapping software to construct mind map from brainstorm of existing knowledge. While in classroom, save it on the college network so that it is available to students for follow-up work.

Take laptop home to prepare web pages and quiz for use on virtual learning environment.

DAY 2

Take laptop into work. In workroom, check e-mail.

Take laptop on visit to student on work placement. Use laptop to record assessment of student using standard forms stored on the laptop. On return from visit, talk to colleague about what I have seen. Transfer assessment records to college network while in colleague's workroom.

Take laptop to meeting of course team. Use it to take minutes there and then. During meeting, download guidance on verification from college network. Retrieve course self assessment from network, update action plan and save back to network. E-mail copy of minutes from laptop to each member of course team and manager.

Talk to colleague about how I have used laptop with students: students have been asking why only some lecturers use laptops to make learning better. Colleague wants one.

Take laptop to classroom. Link to interactive whiteboard to record diagrams drawn on board by group members. Save on laptop to be Incorporated into worksheet later.

In evening class of part-time students, wireless link to network and projector to demonstrate how the college's VLE discussion board works. Set students task of contributing to discussion before following week's session.

Find a secure place to lock up my laptop as I am not taking it home tonight. There is life outside college!

JISC has produced some excellent case studies of how design of spaces for learning is evolving, available through the JISC website. The best new colleges have a clear 'wow' factor when you walk in the front door. What message does that give you as learner – or as a member of staff?

As a result of the first Practical Task for this chapter you will have identified the tools available to you and ones you might use. Write a paragraph or two in your diary or blog about how you might use one or more tools than you currently use. What are the things that are likely to prevent you from doing so? What would your working life be like?

So how do you use these tools?

One of my educational heroines is Donna Brandes, who is strongly identified with student centred learning. Her *Guide to student-centred learning* (Brandes and Ginnis, 1986) is a classic which challenged the way I see the learning process. A while ago, I went to a training course where she gave out a list of what she called 'toes-in tips' for those people who wanted to make their teaching more student-centred but weren't sure where to start. The list included simple tips such as 'sit down with your learners' and ones that needed more preparation such as 'teach and practise listening skills'. I decided to produce a list of toes-in tips for those who wanted to introduce e-learning but aren't quite sure where to start.

PRACTICAL TASK PRACTICAL TASK PRACTICAL TASK PRACTICAL TASK PRACTICAL TASK

Classify the 20 toes-in tips in my list (Table 5.3) into three groups – ones you have used, ones you could use and ones you are unlikely to use. Make a choice of one strategy you have not yet used but could by soon. Plan to use it!

Some of the items in Table 5.3 (page 54) involve putting a bit more than your toe in, but others need little more than a deep breath and a willingness to try things. There is a longer list on the FERL website.

In the rest of the chapter we will look at the same practical ideas for you to use.

Interactive worksheets: such a simple idea...

Much of the software that we use in education and training was not designed for learning; it was intended for office efficiency. Nonetheless, with a bit of creativity, it can make a very effective tool for teachers to use. All you need is a bit of lateral thinking. It's a bit like petrol shortages. If garages put up notices saying. 'You cannot buy more than 20 litres' there will be long queues at petrol stations as motorists try to top up their tanks. If the notices say 'You cannot buy less than 30 litres' motorists would have to use up all they have before buying more, and so no queues. Simple. All you have to do is see it from a different angle and remember your principles of learning.

For example, we know that people learn best when they are doing things and you can create effective interactive activities using a word processor. Here are some examples. The specific instructions are for Microsoft Word 2003, but most word processors have equivalent facilities. If you don't know how to do something specific such as creating text boxes, look it up using the Help menu or ask a colleague.

	have used	could use	wouldn't use
1. Give your learners a list of relevant internet sites to refer to.			
2. Include internet sites in learning activities.			
3. Use the internet as a source of information yourself.			
4. Give your work e-mail address in course leaflets.			
5. Give your work e-mail address to learners (but not your personal address).			
6. Use online discussion groups.			
7. Use PowerPoint presentations.			
8. Ask your learners to give mini PowerPoint presentations.			
9. Make assignments available electronically/ online.			
10. Make learning resources available electronically/online.			
11. Let learners submit assignments electronically.			
12. Use interactive computer programs with your learners.			
13. Encourage learners to word-process assignments.			
14. Encourage learners to use ICT in their assignments.			
15. Support your learners in adapting computers to overcome their learning difficulties and disabilities (e.g. use a spell checker).			
16. Keep records as a spreadsheet/database.			
17. Provide course information on the internet.			
18. Have a course website and display finished work on it.			
19. Make a list of available kit (digital camera, interactive whiteboard, scanner...) and talk to colleagues about how they use it.			
20. Use computer-based tests and quizzes.			

Table 5.3 20 toes-in tips to incorporate e-learning in your teaching

Movable text boxes

Teach your learners how to create and move text boxes and you will have an endless supply of interactive worksheets.

- If your subject involves any sort of sequencing, put each of the steps in a different text box, mix them up on the page and ask your learners to move them into the logical order. I created a geography worksheet showing the stages in the creation of convectional rainfall (see Figure 5.3). Learners had to move them into the order that explained the sequence.
- Put a diagram in the middle of a page with arrows pointing to significant bits. Put appropriate labels in boxes at the bottom of the page. Get learners to move the labels to the correct arrow.
- Write a piece of text in your subject area. Take some words out, for example important technical terms, and put them in separate text boxes at the foot of the page. Ask learners to move the correct term into the correct space. Learners have to work out which is the correct word by understanding the sense of the piece. Make it more thought-provoking for your learners by
  - putting in some extra words as a distraction, so they cannot just work the last ones out by process of elimination;
  - making all the gaps and the text boxes the same size.

Teaching tip

Don't forget to put basic information on every worksheet, interactive or not.

- A title – so you and your learners can identify it.
- A statement of what the learner will learn from completing the worksheet so they know why they are doing it.
- Instructions so the learner knows what to do.
- A footnote at the bottom containing the filename, the date when you created it and your name so that you can find it again in six months' time, consider when you need to update it and lend it to your friends.

Callouts

In Word, a callout is a text box with a pointer on it. Figure 5.4 (page 57) shows some of the different styles of callout in Word. Teach your learners how to use callouts and ask them to annotate diagrams, pictures or maps using them. To insert a callout first make the Drawing toolbar visible (*View → Toolbars → Drawing*) then select *AutoShapes → Callouts →* choose the shape you want. When you move the cursor back to your worksheet, it will become a cross. Click and drag where you want the callout to appear. You can adjust its size by clicking on any of the little box handles and then dragging.

Spell check

For literacy learners needing practice at spelling, show them how to turn the spell checker off and on (*Tools → Options → Spelling and grammar*, then check or uncheck the box marked 'Check spelling as you type'). This will give good repetitious practice at spelling. Make sure you are using the English (UK) dictionary (*Tools → language →* select the correct dictionary language).

Hyperlink to other documents

A hyperlink is a live link, like the ones on the internet that take you to another website. You can link Word documents together using hyperlinks.

- As we discussed in Chapter 3, quick and frequent feedback to learners has a big effect. When you prepare a file containing a worksheet, prepare another file with the answers. Hyperlink the work sheet file to the answer sheet file so that when the learner has worked out an answer, they have the correct answer for comparison. You do have to trust your learners not to cheat, so explain to them how not looking at the answer first will help their learning!

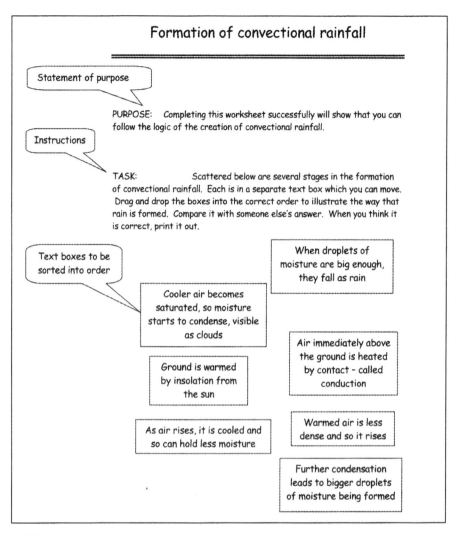

Figure 5.3 Worksheet about the stages in the creation of convectional rainfall

- **In your worksheets, put hyperlinks to other files which contain either extension work for those learners who work more quickly or additional practice for those who move more slowly.**

To put in a hyperlink, go to the hyperlink dialogue box (*Insert → hyperlink*). In the dialogue box, put in the text you want to be the hyperlink (such as 'click here to see the tutor's answer') and *Browse* to find the second file. Don't forget to put a hyperlink on the second file that takes the learner back to their first file. Keep your two files in the same folder.

Word has all sorts of facilities that are potentially useful for creating interactive worksheets, including comments boxes and forms. You can see more suggestions on the ask Butler website. You can do a lot of interactive activities with Excel, too, and there are further examples of that on the same site.

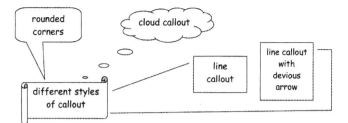

Figure 5.4 Different styles of callout

Teaching tip

Get your learners to create interactive worksheets like these and use them with each other. Keep a stock of the best for use with future groups.

Of course, you do not have to use any of the less well-known facilities in your word processor in order to give your learners things to do. An e-learning worksheet can simply give questions to answer or tasks to do: and the tasks may be:

- at the computer or away from it;
- for an individual learner or more than one learner.

Presentations

PowerPoint is a really useful tool for making presentations, but 'death by PowerPoint' – where the tutor simply reads out what is on the PowerPoint slide for an hour – should be avoided. It never ceases to amaze me that, when I go to conferences on ILT, that is precisely what most presenters do. Why can't they use ILT creatively? Remember learning principles: people learn best when they are doing things and being on the end of a mundane presentation is almost as passive as you can get.

Tips for using PowerPoint more creatively

- **Ask your learners to make and present short PowerPoint presentations. Do this as an alternative to setting written work. Preparing a presentation is an excellent way of learning about a topic and fosters your learners' ICT skills. Delivering the presentation practises communication skills.**
- **Keep some of your learners' presentations and make them available for other groups of learners. Keep good ones to set a standard and keep others with errors in to ask your learners to improve them. You can add a page at the start of each presentation to highlight why it has been kept, as in the following examples.**

  'This presentation is an excellent summary of the main themes. The ideas are presented in an unusual order – but it works!'

  'This presentation includes a good example, but does the conclusion follow from the ideas presented?'

- **Give mini-presentations of no more than 15 minutes (10 is better) on key topics.**
- **Use presentation slides to signpost the sessions you run: show the objectives, signal the start of the next part of the session and show the tasks that learners should be doing.**

- Display a 'thought for the day', which may or may not be about the current topic.
- Incorporate short sound and video clips into your presentations. These may be less than a minute in length but add impact. You probably would not bother to set up a video for only a few seconds of tape.
- Include more in your presentations than bulleted lists. Bulleted lists are good for clarity and structure but can be monotonous.
- Remember the needs of visual learners and include graphics. Pictures, diagrams, graphs and icons all help.
- Include some humour from time to time – for your own sake if not for your learners'.

KISS – Keep It Simple Stupid (nothing personal!) – is very good advice. When you pre-pare presentations, there are design factors to consider. Simplicity and effectiveness often go together.

- Select visual effects carefully for greater impact: only use animations or change font size/type/format if you have a good reason for doing so, not just because you can.
- Think carefully about whether you want the sound effects that come with the animations. In a Windows system turn them off by double-clicking on the loudspeaker icon on the bottom right-hand corner of your screen and checking *'mute all'*.
- Only put a limited amount of text on any one page.
- Make sure text is big enough to read from the back of the room.
- Develop a template so that your presentations look consistent. Remember that when projected onto a screen the colours do not always look the same as on walls – yellow can look good on screen but can be impossible to read when projected. Again, remember the principle of simplicity – blue on a white back-ground looks good. Put a logo on to show ownership.
- Most importantly, choose the right words. Make the words clear, simple and relevant to your learners' needs.

How do you deliver these materials to the learner?

Once you have created these materials you have to deliver them to your learners. How you do this will obviously depend on what facilities you have available.

- If you have a data projector, you could decide that you will deliver as a whole group activity. This might be a good way to do the first activity anyway, so your learners can find out what they need to do.
- If you have access to an interactive whiteboard, get learners to get out of their seats to manipulate the textboxes and other interactive features for themselves. It's a good way to get learners involved and adds a bit of physical movement to the session. Explore the facilities the whiteboard offers, for example to capture different learners' efforts for comparison.
- If you have access to a computer room, learners could each have their own compter. However, don't forget that it is often better for learners to work co-operatively: one learner per computer is not necessarily the ideal.
- If you have a learning centre, your learners can access the materials over the college intranet or network and work on them at a time of their own choosing. Find out whether your learning centre provides tutor support.
- You can make materials available to your learners on CD or USB drive.

For your own peace of mind you should ensure that the materials are protected. A basic protection is to save the files as read-only (*Tools → protect document*). In addition, network systems allow the system administrator to set permissions for who can do what. Typically, for a file storage area where many learners will be accessing the same material, learners would have permission to open files but not to save. If the learner wants to save, they have to do it somewhere else, such as on their own USB drive, or their own personal area. It is also sensible to keep original copies safely out of the way of your learners.

Other materials to make available

Once you have discovered how to put material on your computer network, VLE or intranet, use it to make all sorts of material available to your learners. The materials can be on open access for your learners to browse. Many learners are helped by exploring ideas and materials and resources as the will takes them. It's a bit like using a medical dictionary. You start off looking for a particular condition or symptom, but may not ever find it because you discover other interesting conditions (most of which you are suffering from) on the way.

How about putting some of these on the shared drive, intranet or VLE?

- **Copies of past examination papers.**
- **Examples of work by previous generations of learners; include work with room for improvement as well as good examples.**
- **Checklists of what makes a good examination answer.**
- **A syllabus.**
- **Scheme of work/programme of work.**
- **Examples of self-test questions.**
- **Learner PowerPoint presentations.**
- **Short PowerPoint presentations you have devised.**
- **Interesting newspaper and journal extracts.**
- **Lists of useful websites.**
- **Examiners' reports.**

This would be a good collection for your learners to explore.

Using e-mail

E-mail is a very useful communication tool to use with your learners. Some colleges provide their learners with e-mail accounts; others rely on free services such as Hotmail or Yahoo!. Getting an account is not the major issue influencing the use you can make of e-mail. The main issue is the ability to access the e-mail from home since in 2005–6 fewer than 60 per cent of households have internet connections.

Nonetheless, I find e-mail a very useful tool. I use it for:

- **answering enquiries about my courses (I put my e-mail address in the college prospectus and on publicity leaflets, so initial enquiries often come by e-mail);**
- **sending out initial course information as an attachment;**
- **sending out an enrolment form in an Acrobat (PDF) file as an attachment – the potential learner has to print it out and fill it in because we insist on a signature on the form;**
- **answering queries from course members (I put my work e-mail address in all course handbooks);**
- **submission of assignments by learners (I acknowledge receipt);**
- **chasing up absences (I e-mail to ask why a learner was absent);**
- **attendance information (I ask learners to notify me of a foreseeable absence);**
- **sending the relevant work to learners who miss a class.**

> **Teaching tip**
> In terms of contacting a higher proportion of learners more quickly, texting their mobile phones might be better. Don't forget that calls to mobiles cost more than calls to fixed phones. Text messages can be sent from a computer, to avoid having to do them all separately.

Online discussion

> **PRACTICAL TASK** PRACTICAL TASK PRACTICAL TASK PRACTICAL TASK PRACTICAL TASK
>
> Why would you use discussion in a face-to-face session? Make a list of how discussion helps learning, then compare your list with the ideas that follow.

Face-to-face discussion is an excellent way to foster learning. A group of my colleagues on a training session suggested the following reasons to use discussion.

- **Discussion gives learners the opportunity to explore and demonstrate their subject knowledge.**
- **It helps to build a supportive group and develops social skills.**
- **Learners take ownership of their own learning.**
- **The inclusion of discussion helps meet different learning styles.**
- **Discussion enables learners to articulate and develop thoughts and ideas, and so build their own understanding.**

These same reasons provide the pedagogical justification for selecting online discussion from the teaching toolkit.

Online discussion tools are built into most virtual learning environments. They are also available on the internet, for example at Yahoo! and Smartgroups. As tutor you have decisions to make. Should your discussions be:

- **synchronous or asynchronous;**
- **moderated or unmoderated?**

Synchrononous or asynchronous?
In synchronous discussion the participants are online at the same time. In asynchronous discussion, the participants are online at different times. Although you might think that, because it is immediate, synchronous discussion is best, of the two, asynchronous is the more useful in most circumstances. There are two problems with synchronous discussion. Firstly, agreeing times convenient to all potential participants is often difficult. Secondly, some learners may not be able to keep up with the rate at which faster participants write their messages and may be discouraged. One possible use of synchronous discussion is for tutorials where the tutor is online at a specific time each week.

Asynchronous discussion lets group members participate when they are ready and take their time over what they type. It can make an effective contribution to learning. For example, with courses that run weekly, I set a piece of directed study that requires course members to contribute to online discussion in between the sessions. This keeps them in touch with other learners, breaks down isolation and keeps the momentum of the class going. I also set up discussions to support other aspects of the course, such as the assignments or issues arising from the class sessions. My experience is that course members find the directed study discussions helpful and participate well. It does not always work – I set up an online discussion for members of the Cert Ed (FE) course that ran in my own and three other colleges, and very few people used it. Talking to course members showed that this was because they saw it as an optional add-on and, as such, not essential. Figure 5.5 shows an active discussion group using the WebCT VLE.

Moderated or unmoderated?

In a moderated discussion, all contributions have to be read by a moderator first before they can be seen by everyone else. In an unmoderated discussion, members can post what they want to say directly. Unmoderated discussion is much more spontaneous and has no time delay but there is no control over what is posted. Moderated discussion loses spontaneity but is much more controlled and focused.

The tutor also has to manage the discussion process, which includes:

- **logging on frequently to check contributions;**
- **establishing ground rules for acceptable contributions;**
- **encouraging quiet course members to join in;**
- **discouraging contributions that are over-long;**
- **raising issues to provoke discussion.**

An added bonus provided by online discussion for some learners is that it gives practice with literacy skills. It is very easy to make mistakes when keying in the words, but the emphasis must be on the communication rather than the grammar and spelling errors other contributors make. Contributions to the discussion can also be compiled, printed and put into the learner's Key Skills portfolio of evidence.

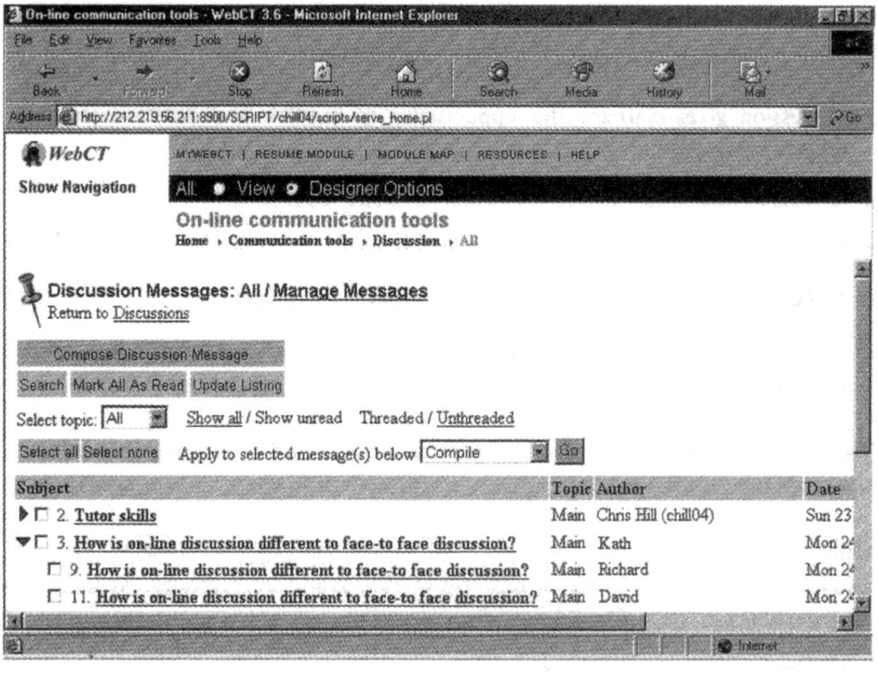

Figure 5.5 A discussion group using WebCT

Web pages

There are other ways besides PowerPoint to present information. One limiting factor with PowerPoint is that it is predominantly designed for linear presentations; in other words, the slides are designed to be accessed in the sequence you thought of when you first set the presentation up. But information is rarely linear, and neither is the need to access it.

A good way round this is to build yourself a website, but instead of putting it on the internet, simply put it on your computer or on a CD and run it offline.The pages in a website are often designed to be accessed in different orders. The pages may be organised in a sequence, but more often they are organised in a hierarchy or as a network. In a hierarchy you start from the home page, which has links to the main sections of the site, and work your way down through sub-pages. In a network you can access almost any page from any other. The pages are connected by hyperlinks.

You might choose to produce all-singing, all-dancing web pages using powerful and pricey software such as Dreamweaver. Alternatively, constructing web pages can be simple and use Word (save as web page) or software easily available on the internet, for example on the Tucows site. You will find several web page editors (referred to as html editors) for you to download. Some are free and others are shareware. Shareware is fully functional software that you can download, try out and decide whether or not it's right for you. If you like it, you pay a nominal fee after the trial period ends. Why is the site called Tucows? Because it uses not a star rating for its software but a cows rating.

The advantages in teaching and learning are significant. I attended a whole-day presentation by a well-known teacher of learning skills. He used a laptop and projector throughout the day and material consisted of a website on his computer which he displayed using his web browser (Internet Explorer – having pressed <FII> to maximise the display size).The home page showed a jumble of 50 or so words that were relevant to the topics that we might be exploring during the day. Clicking on one of the words or phrases took us off to other pages about that topic. Which one he clicked on depended either on choices we made ('Which idea would you like to look at next?') or what he wanted to draw our attention to. The website was simply a big resource that he drew on as he needed. The pages were simple – they consisted of relatively few words and some diagrams.They contained key ideas, significant quotes, activities and lists of resources. The tutor went home having not used most of the material available on his CD, but what he did use was clearly targeted. In essence, it is like taking your entire filing cabinet of resources and work sheets with you to each class you teach.

Webquests

A webquest, according to the Webquest site at the San Diego State University, is an 'inquiry-oriented activity in which some or all of the information that learners interact with comes from resources on the internet'. Webquests can develop thinking skills such as comparing, analysing, classifying, evaluating and deducing. In a webquest you would find:

- an introduction that sets the scene;
- a task that is interesting and doable;
- a list of information sources, including (but not exclusively) internet links;
- a description of what the learners should do;
- guidance on how to use the information acquired;
- a conclusion that brings the quest to a close and focuses on the learning produced.

Webquests can be individual or for learners working together.There are lots of examples on the San Diego site.

Online assessment

We saw in Chapter 3 that feedback is key to effective learning. Computers are very good at giving lots of repetitive practice as often as the learner wants it. There are many programs available for testing learners and letting them establish what they do and do not know. Virtual learning environments all include testing facilities. For example, in Moodle, which is probably the most widely used VLE in the UK, there are many different sorts of tests built in, including:

- multiple choice;
- matching pairs;
- short answer;
- numerical;
- free response.

The computer will happily mark all of these (apart from the free response), give the learner appropriate feedback and give the tutor a record of what the learner has achieved. There are well thought-out routines that alter the order in which the answers in the multiple-choice tests are given so that it reduces the chance of students copying from each other.

There are commercial programs for writing and delivering questions, but the software to use is called Hot Potatoes. Developed by the University of Victoria, it is available free for educational use, provided that the quizzes and tests you create using it are made available to other users. This has the major advantage that, as well as getting an excellent piece of software for nothing, there are many quizzes available for you to use created by other teachers. The FERL website includes an area specifically for users of Hot Potatoes to put a copy of the tests created and so meet the requirement to make tests available to others.

The six different types of tests and quizzes provided by Hot Potatoes are:

- multiple choice;
- short answer;
- fill in the gaps;
- crosswords;
- jumbled sentences;
- matching and mixing.

They are excellent for giving your learners things to do that make them think. And of course you can always get your learners to devise the quizzes and tests for you. They will learn a lot by doing that.

The iPod generation

How many of your learners have iPods or other devices for playing music (generically called MP3 players) permanently plugged into their ears? Do you have your own? They offer much potential for learning because they don't only play music. If you can get your learners to listen to things that relate to their learning, they can listen at any time and in any place – on the bus, walking to classes, during breaks or whilst waiting for something to start. And when they have heard it they can play it again and again until they are sure about it. Believe it or not, if people spend more time learning they generally learn more.

Producing an audio file that can be played on an MP3 player is not difficult. At a minimum you only need a microphone attached to your computer. Windows includes the facility to record sound which works quite satisfactorily for short recordings of a minute or two. For anything longer, it is better to use a specific program, the most common being called Audacity. This is free open source software which enables you to record sound, edit it and convert it into an MP3 file – the form that will play on MP3 players.

How could you use your learners' MP3 players? You could:

- **record the basic ideas in each topic your course covers so your learners can hear them as many times as they want;**
- **record material for learners who prefer an auditory learning style;**
- **record material for learners with visual impairment;**
- **produce a short radio-style programme about the course and the people on it. If you do this regularly, it is called a podcast. It's like having your own radio station;**
- **encourage your learners to produce audio files for each other, or for you as an alternative to making a PowerPoint presentation or writing an essay;**
- **ask an expert to make a short recording for you. I was recruited to make a recording by the PGCE course team at a Shropshire College on why e-learning is important to me.**

And so much more...

That is not it – there's much more. In this chapter I have not tried to cover every single strategy you might use, but rather I have picked those that are more readily available. We have not considered the potential of interactive whiteboards, video conferencing and specialist software or how to get the best out of palmtop computers, personal digital assistants (PDAs), tablet PCs and third-generation mobile phones. New things are emerging all the time. Very few of them are designed primarily for learning, but with the most important tool of all – your imagination – they can all contribute to learning. And creativity and imagination will never go out of date.

REFLECTIVE TASK
REFLECTIVE TASK

Write a paragraph or two in your diary or on your blog on the various strategies in this chapter and how you might use them in your own teaching.

SIGNPOST
In the next chapter we will look at some current priorities in the world of e-learning and ILT.

Visual overview

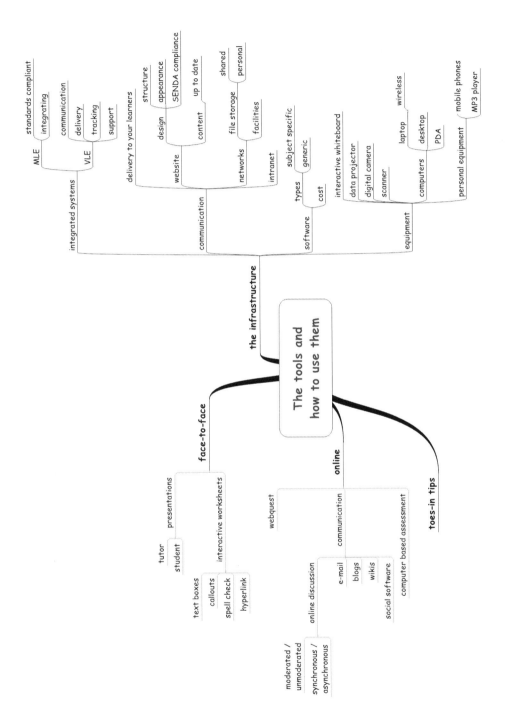

REFERENCES AND FURTHER READING REFERENCES AND FURTHER READING

Phipps, L., Sutherland, A. and Searle, J. (eds) (2002). *Access all areas: disability, technology and learning*. York: TechDis/JISC/Association for Learning Technology.

JISC (2006) *Designing Spaces for Effective Learning*. London: available from the JISC website.

Brandes, D. and Ginnis, P. (1986) *A guide to student-centred learning*. Oxford: Blackwell.

Websites

audacity.sourceforge.net/ Source of the free Audacity sound file editing software FERL resources.

hotpot.uvic.ca Source of the Hot Potatoes assessment software.

uk.groups.yahoo.com/ Facility provided by Yahoo for group networking.

webquest.sdsu.edu/ Webquest site at the San Diego State University.

www.chest.ac.uk Organisation that negotiates software purchasing agreements for HE and FE.

www.edutools.info/ For user reviews of VLEs.

www.hotmail.com Free e-mail system run by Microsoft.

www.jisc.ac.uk/ The JISC website. It is particularly worthwhile to look at the designing spaces case studies of the e-learning innovation programme.

www.learningtechnologies.ac.uk/ask The Ask Butler database of resources, events and examples run by the Learning and Skills Network.

www.moodle.org All about the open source VLE.

www.smartgroups.com/ City and Guilds facility to support its awards.

www.tucows.com/ Exceptional collection of technical resources, ideas and support.

6
Current priorities

This chapter will help you to:

- **locate your use of e-learning amongst national priorities;**
- **consider the value of recent developments;**
- **explore potential use for recently emerging technologies.**

LLUK Standards relevant to this chapter include:
BP3.1, BP5.1, CP3.5.

The first edition of this book was published in 2003. In the relatively short time since then, many things have moved on, including government priorities, the technology itself and how people use it. In this chapter we explore some of the issues that have moved to the top of the agenda now – and some of the things that people believed would be revolutionary and haven't quite made it yet.

The national picture

Amongst a plethora of national publications including the Leitch Report (2006) and the FE White Paper (2007), there have been at least two significant developments for e-learning – the publication of the government's e-strategy (DfES, 2005) and the introduction of mandatory Qualified Teacher Status Learning and Skills (QTLS). *Harnessing Technology* is a statement of the government's e-strategy over the next five years. To the best of my knowledge, it is the only national e-strategy anywhere in the world that covers all ages from pre-school to lifelong learning and universities. The strategy identifies four key areas where ICT and e-learning can contribute to the government's aims for twenty-first century education.

1. Transforming teaching, learning and support.
2. Connecting with hard-to-reach groups.
3. Opening up an accessible, collaborative system.
4. Improving efficiency and effectiveness.

I know that, in reality, strategy is what the government does rather than the plans it puts on paper, but the significance of *Harnessing Technology* is that it firmly emphasises that e-learning is not an option but is at the heart of policy.

I am delighted that qualifications for teachers in the Learning and Skills Sector have become mandatory from September 2007. If children are entitled to trained teachers, why not adults? The plans were first set out in *Equipping our Teachers for the Future* (DfES, 2004) and although that document has few references to e-learning, they are key. In particular, all learners 'must have good, imaginative, modern and relevant teaching (including, for instance, the use of technology to promote personalised learning)'. It required Lifelong Learning UK (LLUK) to ensure that 'the standards for Information and Learning Technologies are integrated' in the standards required of all teachers.

True to this picture, the LLUK Standards contain explicit references to new and emerging technologies. They are shown in Table 6.1. They occur in four of the six domains in the Standards, the only exceptions being Domain A: Professional Values and Practice and Domain F: Access and Progression. Some refer to what teachers know and understand (those with a K in the prefix, e.g. CK3.5) and some refer what teachers do in practice (those with a P in the prefix, e.g. BP3.1). They cover communication skills, resources, support for learners, planning lessons, teaching in your specialist subject, meeting individual learner needs and assessment – a comprehensive list. What's more, in many other standards, e-learning is implicit. For example, what better ways are there to 'engage and motivate learners and encourage independence' (BP2.2) or to 'prepare flexible session plans to adjust to the individual needs of learners' than to use e-learning? If you set up an induction that learners can access online, you clearly 'Provide learners with appropriate information about the organisation and its facilities, and encourage learners to use the organisation's services as appropriate' (FP 1.2).

Domain B: Learning and Teaching

BP 3.1 Communicate effectively and appropriately using different forms of language and media, including written, oral and non verbal communication, and new and emerging technologies to enhance learning.

BP 5.1 Select and develop a range of effective resources, including appropriate use of new and emerging technologies.

Domain C: Specialist Learning and Teaching

CK 3.5 Ways to support learners in the use of new and emerging technologies in own specialist area.

CP 3.5 Make appropriate use of, and promote the benefits of, new and emerging technologies.

Domain D: Planning for Learning

DP 1.2 Plan teaching sessions which meet the aims and needs of individual learners and groups, using a variety of resources, including new and emerging technologies.

Domain E: Assessment for Learning

EK 1.2 Ways to devise, select, use and appraise assessment tools, including where appropriate those which exploit new and emerging technologies.

EP 1.2 Devise, select, use and appraise assessment tools, including where appropriate those which exploit new and emerging technologies.

Table 6.1 Reference to new technology in the LLUK Standards

Equipping our teachers also demanded that all teacher training teams model effective practice in the use of new and emerging technologies and offer courses using a blended approach. When all new teachers and trainers experience e-learning for themselves we will be getting there.

A term that keeps cropping up in relation to e-learning is embedding. The use of new technology must be embedded in the practice both of individual teachers and of the organisations they work for. What does embedding mean? A useful definition is that a technology is embedded when you can't think of doing your job without it. QTLS should mean that many more teachers have e-learning embedded in their toolkit. At least, it will if teacher training teams get their act together to model effective practice.

VLEs and blended learning

A further area where significant progress has been made is the use of Virtual Learning Environments and blended learning. When I wrote the first edition of this book, many FE colleges had a VLE because they had been given money to buy one, but in very few were they used for anything other than delivering the occasional distance learning course where an enthusiast had set things going. Now, senior managers have become much more interested in a VLE as a delivery tool – and not just one to save money. The emphasis is on improving the quality of learning for each individual and engaging hard-to-reach groups – the key e-learning advantages of personalisation and accessibility. We are getting to understand better the mix between e-learning and traditional learning – blended learning. In fact, in some organisations, the VLE is becoming embedded; you can't imagine doing your job without it.

So what does a VLE do? Here are some of the functions that most VLEs can carry out. A VLE will:

- **deliver course documentation;**
- **provide a course overview;**
- **structure and sequence learning;**
- **deliver learning activities;**
- **make resources available, including internet resources;**
- **communicate between learner and tutor;**
- **communicate between learners;**
- **assess learners and provide feedback;**
- **monitor learner experience.**

PRACTICAL TASK PRACTICAL TASK PRACTICAL TASK PRACTICAL TASK PRACTICAL TASK

For a course that you deliver, explore which of these VLE functions would be useful to you. What would you gain or lose if the VLE carried out that function? You may find the sections in Chapter 2 on reasons for using e-learning and the examples of blended learning helpful.

In the region in which I work, many learning providers are switching to Moodle as their VLE. Moodle is an example of open source software, which is software released under an Open Source Initiative (OSI) certified licence. There are ten conditions for such a licence, including free redistribution of the software, access to the source code (its internal workings) and permission to modify it. It's a brilliant example of the community getting together to share knowledge and expertise. And with Moodle, it really works. If you want Moodle to do something it wasn't originally designed to do, you can almost guarantee that someone, somewhere will have already done it and will share it with you. If you have a problem, someone will have already solved it – and if they have the same problem, they could be willing to work with you to sort it out. You can see the online community on the Moodle website and there are Moodle Users groups in most regions, such as those run by the JISC Regional Support Centres. Other examples of commonly used open source software are the Firefox web browser (an alternative to Internet Explorer) and Open Office, an alternative to Microsoft Office. The best source of information on open source software is the JISC service OSS Watch.

Teaching tip

If you like the mind maps included in this book, there is an open source program for drawing them available called Freemind. Download it from http://freemind.sourceforge.net and encourage your learners to try it. The significance of a mind map is not so much the finished product, but how it lets you reorganise your thoughts during the process of creating it.

Personalisation

Personalisation is the focus of much current attention in the Learning and Skills sector. It features strongly in *Harnessing Technology*. The first of the Quality Improvement Agency's priority actions in *Pursuing Excellence: the National Improvement Strategy for the Further Education System* (QIA, 2007) is to embed personalisation and increase the learner voice. The FE White Paper (DfES, 2006) highlights the need for 'increasing personalisation, so that individual needs and circumstances are built into the design and delivery of education and training'. That is one working definition of personalisation – and e-learning has a very clear role to play in it.

BECTA (2007) has drawn up a discussion paper on the role of new technology in personalising learning. It identifies the essential characteristics of personalisation as 'inclusion; choice and preference; engagement and participation; responsiveness; flexibility; tailored and adaptable; and independence' – all of which feature as benefits of new technology. Some of these require significant planning, time and investment, and are outside the scope of the individual teacher, whereas others are achievable to you as an individual teacher with your current learners. Amongst the former are:

- **opening up opportunities for learning to a greater range of learners and lifestyles such as the housebound, those in rural areas or shift workers;**
- **building links between formal and informal learning;**
- **making records of assessment and progress available to those who need them in a format that is understandable.**

What can you do as a teacher with your current learners? The answer is – lots! For example, you could:

- **encourage learners to reflect on their progress by giving them lots of online assessments with instant feedback;**
- **get your learners to help design parts of their curriculum such as resources, quizzes (with answers!) and activities;**
- **set up online discussion groups and mailing lists to create networks of learners;**
- **give learners choices as to which way they present their work – for example as a PowerPoint presentation, word-processed essay or sound file.**

REFLECTIVE TASK

Make a list of actions you could take to introduce a higher degree of personalisation into your teaching. Download the discussion paper from the Becta website and decide what opportunities are open to you as an individual teacher and which would require the involvement of your colleagues.

At this point it is worth pointing out that the concept of personalisation is still evolving. Whilst on one hand you might see it, in line with the above DfES definition, as customising what you do as a teacher to meet the needs of each learner, perhaps it is more to do with giving ownership and control to the learner. We are back to the idea that learning belongs to the learner and not the teacher; it is something you do and not something that is done to you. There is also the danger that personalisation goes hand in hand with individualism, whereas for me and I suspect many people, learning is a social activity.

Web 2.0

There is a feeling that the world wide web is entering a new phase in its development – web 2.0 – although others (including Tim Berners-Lee, the father of the web) argue that it is simply going back to its roots as a device for sharing and collaborating. There has been an explosion of exotically named tools including YouTube, MySpace, wikis and blogs. Web 2.0 is not about new technologies and tools, but about changes in the way that people are using the web. The characteristics include:

- **content generated by the users; much of the web has been about downloading content that other people put there. With web 2.0 it is about contributing as much as receiving;**
- **relying on the knowledge and understanding of others, the collective wisdom;**
- **huge amounts of data being made available;**
- **openness and sharing.**

The implications for education and training are still emerging, although there are already many examples of creative and effective use. In Table 6.2, I set out some of the tools that you might be able to use with your learners. It is based on categories from a JISC Technology and Standards Watch report on web 2.0 technologies which is well worth exploring (Anderson, 2007). A further source to set you thinking is the Future Lab publication *Social software and learning* (Owen, Grant, Sayers and Facer, 2006).

Your learners will already make extensive use of some of these tools. You could decide to take advantage of this on the basis that they are the means of communication your learners value and are familiar with. However, you will probably find that, by the time you have learned about the latest tool, your learners will have moved on from it or, if not, they resent you intruding into their world. The trick is to get your learners to suggest to you how they can use them.

Many web 2.0 tools such as blogs and wikis are available within a VLE such as Moodle. It is all very well to put them into courses that you design, but you will have to encourage learners to use them. The best ways to do this is either to make them part of the formal assessment or work hard to help your learners understand how the tool helps learning.

PRACTICAL TASK PRACTICAL TASK PRACTICAL TASK PRACTICAL TASK PRACTICAL TASK

For one of the web 2.0 tools in Table 6.2, discuss its possible use with your learners. What would it offer you and them? What would you have to give up in order to use it?

Category	Example	Description	Potential learning use
blogs	www.blogger.com	an online journal where its owner posts contributions and others can respond with comments	• a diary reflecting on something you are reading (like this book) or on work experience. The author can choose to share it with the tutor or fellow learners • progress record on solving a problem
wikis	www.wikipedia.org	web page or set of web pages that can be easily edited or added to by anyone who has access to them	• learners share prior knowledge before starting a new topic • each learner contributes a small section they have researched to build up a whole picture
tagging and social bookmarking	www.furl.net del.icio.us	systems for labelling and sharing things that you find on the web, like your 'favorites'	• groups of learners can share useful websites relevant to the topic being studied • learners can build up a shared resource of revision websites
multimedia sharing	www.youtube.com www.flickr.com	store and share multimedia content such as video (YouTube) and pictures (Flickr)	• a creative alternative to present what is known in video format • a picture gallery related to study area
audio blogs and podcasting	www.impala.ac.uk	sound recordings designed to be heard on a computer or portable MP3 player. Now can incorporate video – a vodcast	• tutor prepared summary of key points in study topic • learner prepared application of (economics) principles to current events
RSS and syndication	www.bbc.co.uk	Really Simple Syndication – a system for bringing a synopsis of newly published web content to your desktop	• learners access RSS feeds on subject relevant sites • learners prepare brief newsletter using material from RSS feeds
social networking	www.myspace.com www.facebook.com	sites which facilitate the sharing of content and meeting other people virtually	• again, a creative alternative to presenting information • create a study group to provide mutual support

Table 6.2 Some easily available web 2.0 tools

Not quite there yet

1. Video conferencing

One of the difficulties of new technology is that it is new. Until it becomes established, it is hard to judge what is going to be useful and what not. We have just moved house and doing so revived the delights of a variety of technologies that are now redundant – for example, reel to reel tape recorder, cassette tape walkman, CD walkman and minidisk player. They all still work so it seems wrong to abandon them.

In the experience of most learners in the Learning and Skills sector, video conferencing is a technology that has never quite achieved the significance that was predicted for it and would end up at the back of the cupboard. Where it has been used with success there tends to be limited interaction – typically a presentation by an acknowledged expert who then responds to questions from the widely distributed audience. However, other more accessible tools emerge with changing technology and some will stick. Video conferencing on a personal scale works very effectively using free tools such as Skype. If your computer is equipped with a web cam (cost from £12) and an earphones/microphone headset (cost from £6) you can have clear conversations enhanced by being able to look at the person you are talking to. You could use this for one-to-one tutorials.

There are other ways of web conferencing – delivering voice and pictures over the internet – that are worth investigating.

- **JISC Legal delivers a series of webcasts on legal issues around e-learning. The webcast on copyright is particularly helpful.**
- **TechDis has been experimenting with a number of web conferencing tools, especially Instant Presenter. Search for 'web conferencing' on the TechDis website to see what they have learned.**
- **You can add video and sound such as a tutor commentary to your PowerPoint presentations using a free download from the Microsoft website called Producer. There is a good case study from Fermanagh College in 'Effective practice with e-learning' (JISC, 2004).**

2. e-portfolios

Work on e-portfolios divides into two. Concept 1 sees the e-portfolio as an electronic collection of evidence of competence in a vocational qualification, especially an NVQ. The role of the e-portfolio is to avoid the collection of vast amounts of paper evidence of competence. A Learning and Skills Council pilot study of computerised assessment shows that as much as £1 billion a year is being wasted on duplicated effort and paperwork associated with NVQs and related vocational courses where assessment involves the collection of evidence of competence (source: ferl). There are a number of available commercial tools including QuickStep, Learning Assistant and OneFile.

Concept 2 sees the e-portfolio as a support for lifelong learning. In its extreme form it gathers together your formal education, employment and leisure activities to build a picture that you take with you throughout your learning life. In practice, it is about progression from one stage of education to the next or progress within an award. This version has much further to go.

Whilst it seems a good idea that when you start a new course in a new place, you take with you a record of all your experience and achievement, so you can gain recognition of your prior learning, in practice there are a number of issues.

- **The technology to do this is not yet clear. How is the data held? Is it in one huge database held centrally? Is it in lots of different co-ordinated databases? What standards do there have to be to allow data to be passed from one organisation to another?**

- The ownership of the data needs to be established. Do I own my own data or is it owned by someone else. If someone else owns it, can I control who sees it? I might not want my new organisation to know all about my past. Can I edit things out that I want to keep secret? One of the traditional advantages of going to an FE college is to start again and leave your mistakes behind you.
- Who pays the cost of the e-portfolio? Would those who cannot afford it be at a disadvantage?

Nonetheless, there are some encouraging aspects to e-portfolios although there is no grand overall system emerging, despite some good intentions. At best, there are local developments which establish models and things that work – or not. You can explore the current state of development in the e-learning focus part of the JISC website. The Loughborough e-Progress File case study is particularly interesting.

3. e-assessment

E-assessment offers potential advantages over traditional forms of assessment, including speed of marking, speed of receiving feedback, the chance to repeat assessments until the learner is confident of what has been learned and possibly even fun with less stress for the respondent. Computer marking is neutral and objective: a computer won't put you down if you get something wrong. For many learners this is preferable to marking by a person. The key issue is that computers can mark some sorts of questions but not others. They can do repetitive multiple choice tests or practice mathematical calculations until the cows come home. What they are not so good at is marking free response.

PRACTICAL TASK PRACTICAL TASK PRACTICAL TASK PRACTICAL TASK PRACTICAL TASK

See if you can construct some multiple choice questions that can test higher order skills such as evaluation or synthesis, rather than simple skills such as remembering or recognising. If you find this difficult in your subject area – and it probably is – you will see how tempting it is to only assess those things that are easy to assess rather than the things that ought to be assessed.

Computers can be really powerful in administration of assessment. I currently lead a team of markers on a GCSE geography paper for an awarding body. Candidates write their answers in the normal way but then they are scanned in and marking is done online. In lots of ways marking is more accurate. For example:

- as markers only mark parts of questions rather than whole scripts, any one candidate's work is marked by several markers so differences between generous, mean and even erratic markers balance themselves out;
- one in every 20 or so responses has already been marked by senior examiners so I can see where my markers are not marking to the standard required;
- the computer makes far fewer mistakes in adding up the marks than human markers.

REFLECTIVE TASK

Write a paragraph or two in your diary or on your blog about the various ideas in this chapter and how they relate to your own teaching.

There is an instructive introduction to e-assessment on the TechDis website – put e-assessment in the search box.

SIGNPOST▶ In the next chapter we will explore the range of skills that you need to exploit the potential of ILT and how you can develop those skills.

Visual overview

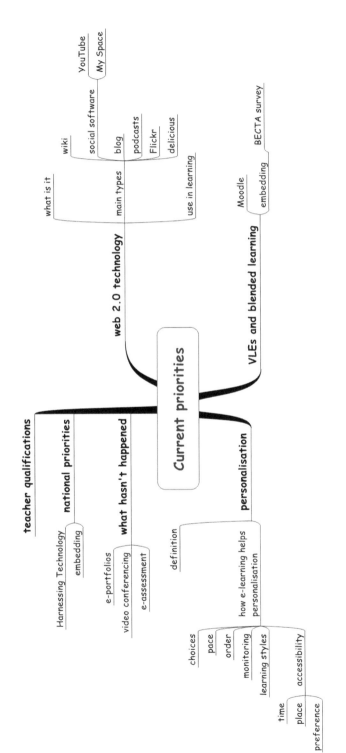

REFERENCES AND FURTHER READING REFERENCES AND FURTHER READING

Anderson, P. (2007) *What is Web 2.0? Ideas, technologies and implications for education*. JISC Technology and Standards Watch; downloadable from http://www.jisc.ac.uk/media/documents/techwatch/tsw0701b.pdf

BECTA (2007) *Personalising Learning: The Opportunities Offered by Technology* downloadable from learningandskills.becta.org.uk/display.cfm?resID=31571

DfES (2005) *Harnessing Technology*. London: downloadable from www.dfes.gov.uk/publications/e-strategy/

DfES (2006) *FE Reform: Raising Skills, Improving Life Chances*. London: downloadable from www.dfes.gov.uk/publications/furthereducation/

HM Treasury (2006) *Prosperity for all in the global economy – world class skills: The Leitch Report*. London: downloadable from www.hmtreasury.gov.uk/media/6/4/leitch_finalreport051206.pdf

JISC (2004) *Effective practice with e-learning*. London: JISC. Downloadable from www.jisc.ac.uk/elp_practice.html

LLUK (2007) *New professional standards for teachers, tutors and trainers in the lifelong learning sector* downloadable from *www.lifelonglearninguk.org*

Owen, M., Grant, L., Sayers, S. and Facer, K. (2006) *Social software and learning*. Bristol: Learning Lab downloadable from www.futurelab.org.uk/research/opening_education.htm

QIA (2007) *Pursuing Excellence* downloadable from www.qia.org.uk/pursuingexcellence/resources.html

Websites

http://freemind.sourceforge.net You can download free, open source, mind mapping software from here.

http://moodle.org/ Website of the Moodle organisation.

www.elearning.ac.uk/mle/cases The Loughborough college e-progress file case study.

www.jisclegal.ac.uk/ The JISC legal website which contains a number of good webcasts. Follow the webcast link.

www.microsoft.com Source of MS Producer. To download it, either enter 'Producer' in the search box or follow the links to the Download Center (sorry!).

www.oss-watch.ac.uk/ Website of OSSwatch, the JISC funded service which specialises in open source software.

www.skype.com Tools for computer to computer voice and picture communication.

www1.onefile.co.uk; www.ctdquickstep.co.uk; www.learningassistant.com/ Providers of e-portfolio systems.

7
The skills you need

This chapter will help you to:

- **identify the skills you need for effective use of e-learning;**
- **audit your own e-learning skills;**
- **select strategies for developing appropriate skills.**

LLUK Standards relevant to this chapter include:
BP3.1, CP3.5, EK1.2.

Running through this book is a theme that says adopting e-learning does not mean abandoning our existing teaching skills – it revitalises them. E-learning does not alter what is important in learning: it is simply another set of tools in the teaching and learning toolkit. As a teacher using e-learning, you need teaching skills and knowledge of learners and the learning process – the same knowledge and understanding all teachers need. If you can add a sprinkling of creativity, then so much the better.

In this chapter we will set out the skills you need for effective ILT use, give you the tools to evaluate your current level of skills and suggest some ways of acquiring the appropriate skills.

A Professional Development Framework for e-learning

If the use of e-learning is implicit in many of the LLUK Standards, it could be helpful to have the e-learning skills needed by teachers, tutors and trainers – and their managers – made explicit. The Learning and Skills Network, together with the Centre for Excellence in Leadership and the Learning and Skills Council, have published a framework to help with this (LSN, 2007). Its prime purpose is to be a tool for managing professional development, but it does include very useful lists of competences of e-learning skills, with learning outcomes and criteria.

The Framework provides you with a map of the e-learning territory that the teacher operates within. Few teachers will operate in every aspect listed, but the framework gives a standard for comparison.

- **For learning providers, the Framework helps directly in recruitment and management of staff and their professional development.**
- **For the individual teacher, the Framework can play a key role in professional development. The competencies let you establish your present skills, attributes and knowledge and make decisions about what to focus on next. You can decide which areas of the map are your strength and which areas are not so strong, and plan your development accordingly.**

1. E-learning fundamentals
2. Initial/diagnostic assessment, induction and guidance
3. Blended learning
4. Use of learning environments, platforms and online learning
5. Choosing and using content
6. Assembling and adapting content
7. Assessment, tracking and e-portfolios
8. Supporting learners to use e-learning and technology
9. Online learning, coaching, mentoring and developing peer support
10. Exploring the application of e-tools
11. Undertake an e-learning development project

Table 7.1 The main topic headings for practitioners in the ePD Framework

Table 7.1 shows the main topic headings in the Framework for practitioners. There are further topics for e-learning developers, those who lead e-learning and for those who advise on e-learning.

Do not assume, however, that you must develop areas you regard as a weakness. Only decide to develop them if they are relevant to your present and expected roles. It may make better sense to concentrate your professional development on your strengths. The analogy is David Beckham and the full range of football skills. It would be a waste of time to work on developing his goalkeeping skills, even though goalkeeping is one of the roles in playing football. He should concentrate on his strengths, especially accurate passing to team mates long distances away. He has exceptional awareness of where players are; I wonder if he is a spatial learner?

REFLECTIVE TASK

Use the Professional Development Framework for e-learning as the basis of assessing your own e-learning competence and planning to develop your skills.

1. Obtain a copy of the Framework. Read through the topic areas in Table 7.1 and decide which you want to focus on, then look up the relevant competences in the Framework.

2. Write a paragraph or two in your diary or on your blog on your strengths and which Standards you would like to target for your professional development. Set goals and action plan how you will achieve them.

3. Repeat this activity every six months or so as the basis of your on-going professional development in e-learning.

Online tutoring skills

Classroom teaching is all about establishing relationships between teacher and learner and between learners. Communication skills are critical in that process. Similarly, online learning depends upon establishing good relationships if it is to be effective. Transferring face-to-face teaching skills to the online setting needs thought and reflection. It requires more than simply writing down the things you would say face to face.

PRACTICAL TASK PRACTICAL TASK PRACTICAL TASK PRACTICAL TASK PRACTICAL TASK

What forms of communication take place in face-to-face communication that do not happen online? What do you think is the consequence of these forms, of communication not being available?

The forms of communication that are absent from online learning, such as tone of voice and body language, refine and reinforce the words used. The meaning of words on their own is much less certain. To try this out, find how many different meanings you can make for the word 'no' simply by changing the tone of your voice. It can mean amazement, a question, a definite no, a possible no or even, under some circumstances, a yes.

Salmon (2000) identifies five areas in which 'e-moderators' (her term for those managing online discussion) need competencies.

1. An understanding of the online process – you need to know how the process works and how it creates learning.
2. Technical skills – you need to be comfortable in the operation of the software yourself and also in enabling learners to use it.
3. Online communication skills – you need not only to be able to communicate effectively but to engage with your learners.
4. Content expertise – you need to be a better subject expert as an e-moderator because it is much less predictable than, for example, a lecture. Consequently it is not as safe. A lecture – especially if you do not let your learners get a word in edgeways – is much more predictable. Your content expertise must extend to internet resources.
5. Personal characteristics – you need to be sensitive, confident, enthusiastic and motivated.

To develop the skills of an e-moderator, it is probably useful to have the experience of being an online learner.There is an increasing number of online qualifications available about online learning, including the Sheffield College's Learning to Teach Online (LeTTOL). The Joint Examining Board, now part of Education Development International, offers both the Certificate in the Educational Use of the Internet and the Certificate in Delivering Learning using a VLE. All of these aim to develop the skills of online delivery. You might prefer to choose a course about something other than online learning. Alternatively, you might simply join in online discussion groups such as those hosted by Google. This will give you practice at writing appropriately for online communication and reading other people's contributions. Sometimes they will get it wrong and you will be able to learn from that.

Courses about online learning do not have to be big. I have just completed an Open University course to train e-moderators based around Salmon's book (2000). It was planned to only be upwards of four hours of learning, which our group of ten learners tackled over two weeks. Despite its brevity, I have learned once again how strong a relationship can develop between online course members.

Materials development skills

Another aspect of transferring your traditional learning skills to the online context is in the development of learning materials. Even though the National Learning Network is investing considerable amounts of money in providing learning materials, some of which are all-singing, all-dancing, most teachers will still want to produce some materials for themselves. You have an ownership (although not necessarily copyright) of materials you produce, and they can be specifically targeted at precisely what you want and your students need.

FERL Practitioners' Programme

One good opportunity that may be available to you to develop your ILT skills is the FERL Practitioners' Programme. The FERL website says that the FERL Practitioners' Programme has

> *been created to equip those individuals involved in the teaching and learning process in colleges with the skills essential for harnessing the potential of ILT. It is designed for delivery within colleges, facilitated by college staff using materials designed by the FERL team at BECTA.*

It is designed to meet the needs both of complete beginners and those who draw up and implement college ILT strategies. This in itself is quite a challenge. Colleges can choose to use the sections that are relevant to their own staff development needs. It concentrates on teaching and learning issues rather than technology.

The full version, launched in the spring of 2003, consists of five strands. These are:

Strand I – Using ILT with learners;
Strand 2 – Assisting and supporting staff to use ILT with learners;
Strand 3 – Making ILT happen in teaching and learning;
Strand 4 – Learning On-line: the use of learning platforms and virtual learning environments;
Strand 5 – The contribution of technical staff to teaching and learning.

The material is not only relevant to colleges but to any learning provider in the Learning and Skills Sector. Whether or not your organisation uses any of the FERL Practitioner Programme materials, you could find them helpful.

The ICT skills you need

Although the teaching and learning skills are the most important, to be an effective e-learning tutor, you do have to have a basic competence in ICT. Essentially, you need to know enough to do what you want to do: you do not have to be a technical expert. There are a number of audits that enable you to check your own ICTskills. Among the most comprehensive is the list produced by BECTA of the skills that ILT Champions need. Remember that the Champions are not 'champions' in that they are expected to be technical experts; they are champions as in enthusiasts or evangelists, so the people skills are more important. You can download the Champion audit from the FERL website.

What technical skills are required? Table 7.2 lists the skills I would identify as the foundation ones you need, although, of course, this will depend on the context you work in. There is no point in worrying about having lots of skills that relate to using a computer network when you only have access to stand-alone computers. The list assumes you are using a Windows-based computer, but can be adapted to other sorts.

PRACTICAL TASK PRACTICAL TASK **PRACTICAL TASK** PRACTICAL TASK **PRACTICAL TASK**

For each of the items in the audit in Table 7.2 (page 82), put a tick under the relevant column showing whether you can do it completely, in part, or not at all. Write a paragraph or two in your diary or on your blog on your strengths and devise an action plan for the skills you would like to develop. You might also identify those things you can do but do not always bother with, such as backing up your files.

I carried out a fuller version of this audit with a sample of the academic staff in my own college and found that:

- women scored higher than men;
- part-time teachers scored higher than full-time teachers;
- the strongest skills were in use of e-mail and word processing;
- only one in five could set up a data projector;
- many staff had limited housekeeping skills, especially file management.

I wonder how typical these findings are? I aim to repeat the audit to see whether skills have progressed.

Teaching tip

Identify a list of the ICT skills you expect your learners to have. Find out how your learners can develop the skills they need. Talk to colleagues and, if appropriate, the person in your organisation who is responsible for key skills or student entitlement.

Housekeeping skills

Skills that often get overlooked are housekeeping skills – the ability to work in a neat and tidy, organised way. Ask yourself the following questions.

- Can you always find a file you created six months ago?
- Are you short of file storage space because you have lots of files you will never, ever use again?
- If one of your files becomes corrupted or damaged, do you have a copy available?

When learning word processing, most people learn it a bit at a time, as they need to do it. You want to centre a heading so you ask a colleague how to do it, you explore the icons and menus in your word-processing program, or, when all else fails, you look it up using the Help menu. You learn when you need to do it – it is 'just in time' learning, and, as such, very effective – people learn best when they need to learn. But you are only aware of housekeeping skills when something goes wrong – for example, when you have a list of 100 files called 'document' to 'document100' and cannot find the one you need. Follow these useful principles.

- Give files long names that make sense now and will also make sense in six months' time.
- Organise your files into folders. Create lots of folders for all the different aspects of your work. Create folders within folders.
- Every so often, go through your files and tidy them up. Make sure files are in the appropriate folder. Delete files you will never need again.
- Regularly take backup copies of your files so that if something goes wrong (and you can be sure it will at some point) you do not lose important documents.

Skills	Can do	Some skill	Cannot do
Underpinning knowledge			
• define terms: hardware; software; peripheral; operating system; application			
• identify the main components of a computer system and explain the functions of each one			
• explain basic computer concepts in non-technical terms			
• use Help menus to learn about what you don't know			
• explain health and safety requirements for using computers			
Kit			
• set up a data projector			
• connect and install a new piece of kit, e.g. a scanner			
Housekeeping your computer			
• organise your files in folders			
• copy, move, delete and rename files			
• regularly backup your files, just in case			
Word process			
• create, save, save as and open documents			
• save document as a web page			
• format text (e.g. centre, bold and headings), including use of styles			
• insert graphics into a document			
• insert tables			
• put document details such as the document name and the date you created it in a footer (so you can find it next time)			
• create templates			
E-mail			
• create and send e-mails			
• sort your e-mails into folders			
• send e-mails to groups of people			
• attach files – and open attachments when you receive them			
Presentations			
• create and deliver a presentation			
• include graphics, video, sound and hyperlinks in a presentation			

Skills	Can do	Some skill	Cannot do
Internet			
• go directly to an internet address by typing it in			
• add addresses to your favorites (sic)/bookmarks			
• save internet pages			
• copy text or graphics from a web page			
• search using at least two search engines			
• download files from the internet (e.g. pdf files)			
Social web use			
• create and write a blog			
• record an audio file			
• make it available as a podcast			
• set up and contribute to a wiki			
Peripherals			
• scan a picture			
• scan text and transfer it into your word processor			
• take a picture on a digital camera or mobile phone and transfer it into your computer			
• use a graphics program to adjust the picture, e.g. alter the size			
• take a short video on a digital camcorder and transfer it to a computer			
• create a CD or DVD using a CD or DVD re-writer			

Table 7.2 ICT skills audit

Health and safety skills

Health and Safety is clearly something that other people have to worry about: it never applies to you.

- **Other people should take a break from working too long at the computer, but you just need to finish the piece of work you are doing.**
- **Other people should make sure they have a decent chair, but you will just use this low chair because it is here and it is not worth fetching an adjustable one.**
- **It would be better if the light from the window was not reflected in this computer screen, but that means the bother of moving the kit around so it faces the other way or asking for (or even worse, paying for) proper blinds.**

I know – I have done all these things, and more, and it is not clever: it is simply irresponsible. You must look after your own health and it is vital that you model the sort of behaviour you want from your learners. If you model poor practice, your learners will certainly pick that up. Learning health and safety is only in part about knowledge. More than anything it is about attitudes and values and you cannot teach attitudes and values simply by telling.

Developing your technical skills

If you decide that developing your ICT skills is a priority, most colleges offer appropriate courses. You might choose to go for a complete qualification such as the European Computer Driving Licence (ECDL). ECDL is a European-wide qualification that aims to develop computer competence across seven areas. These are:

1. basic concepts of IT;
2. using the computer and managing files;
3. word processing;
4. spreadsheets;
5. database;
6. presentation;
7. information and communication.

You do not have to take the whole qualification, you can select the part that is relevant for you. Section 2 is particularly good for developing housekeeping skills.

The OCR qualification Computer Literacy and Information Technology (CLAIT) has now been updated and is a popular alternative, with the advantage that it is available in three levels. It also can include Microsoft Office. If you are starting completely from scratch, you could try BBC Webwise. It can also be part of New CLAIT.

Rather than tackling a broad range of skills through a general qualification, you may want to develop specific ones. Here, Learndirect courses are worth a look. Most of the courses can be done online from home or from a Learndirect centre, and they typically take a small number of hours.

There are some ICT skills courses specifically designed for teachers, such as the JEB level 3 Certificate in the Educational Use of IT. Here, you do not simply learn how to word-process a document, but to produce a worksheet or a handout.

Teaching tip

(A learning tip rather than a teaching one.) Most ICT courses do not assume you are working in education. To get the maximum benefit from taking them, make sure you spend some time thinking through how you can apply your new skills to the teaching and learning context, as set out in the Kolb experiential learning cycle (see Chapter 3).

Your creativity

I hope that you are now enthusiastic to develop your skills so you can take advantage of the potential benefits of ILT. But into the mix of skills, don't forget to add the spice of creativity. I attended a day-long training event in London where the organisers promised us a learning styles toolkit to meet the needs of physical learners. What they actually gave us was two packets of clothes pegs and a metre-long strip of Velcro. And it worked. What is your equivalent to pegs and Velcro?

REFLECTIVE TASK
REFLECTIVE TASK

Write a paragraph or two in your diary or on your blog about your level of e-learning skills, the level you would like them to be at and how you will achieve that.

GNPOST Skills on their own are not enough. You also need effective resources. The resources on the internet are one of the strongest arguments for adding ILT to your teaching toolkit. In the next chapter we will explore those resources – how to find good ones and link them to your teaching.

REFERENCES AND FURTHER READING
REFERENCES AND FURTHER READING

LSN (2007) *A professional development framework for e-learning*. London: LSN.
Salmon, G. (2000) *E-moderating: the key to teaching and learning online*. London: Kogan Page.

Websites
ferl.qia.org.uk/ Further Education Resources for Learning
www.jeb.co.uk/ Joint Examining Board
www.learndirect.co.uk/ Learndirect
www.learningtechnologies.ac.uk/ LearningTechnologies
www.sheffcol.ac.uk/lettol/ Learning to Teach On-line information is available on the Sheffield College website
www.nln.ac.uk/ National Learning Network
www.bbc.co.uk/webwise/ Webwise

Visual overview

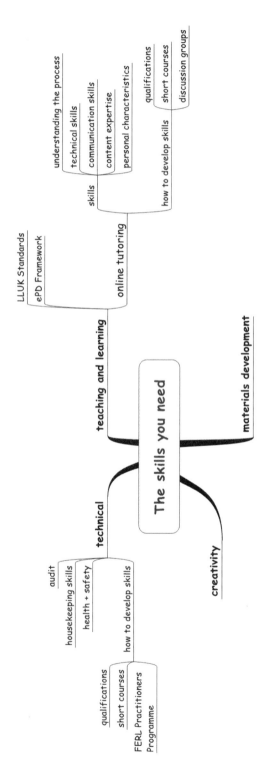

8
e-learning resources

This chapter will help you to:

- **find internet resources;**
- **identify resources relevant to your subject;**
- **identify resources to support teaching and learning;**
- **evaluate internet resources.**

LLUK Standards relevant to ths chapter include:
BP5.1, DP1.2.

Almost everything you need in the way of information is on the internet. Somewhere, there is probably exactly what you want, if only you can find it. Searching is an important skill and we start this chapter by looking at how you can increase the efficiency of your searching. We will then explore some of the materials and services explicitly provided for e-learning in the further education sector. We end by considering issues relating to using internet resources with your learners.

Finding what you want on the world wide web

You can explore the internet for a long time without finding anything of use at all. Browsing – simply following links from one web page to another – is fun, but it relies on serendipity to produce anything useful. It's the medical dictionary again – never actually finding what you started off looking for because you have found something else on the way.

Teaching tip

Browsing can be a very effective way to find subject resources if you start from the right place. My wife, who has compiled a very impressive list of websites to support her teaching of classical civilisation, started by simply browsing from one or two subject-specific sites, using the links she found there. You can find the site to start from by talking to colleagues who teach your subject, by reading a subject-interest journal – in this example published by the Joint Association of Classical Teachers – or by using a search engine.

Although browsing from a good starting point can be effective, searching will have wider coverage. Although often lumped together under the heading of 'search engines', there are three types of search facility which, with a bit of thought, will find you what you want.

- **Search engines such as Google** (www.google.com/) **and Alta Vista** (uk.altavista.com/). **Search engines are huge databases containing details of millions of web pages. They are created by software called a spider or a crawler, which automatically visits web pages, indexes what it finds there, follows any links to the other web pages and starts the process again. There is no quality control to this and no guarantee about the worth of what the crawler finds.**
- **Web directories such as Yahoo!** (http://uk.yahoo.com/). **These are hierarchical lists of internet resources, sorted by topic. Unlike search engines, they are compiled by editors who select and categorise the web pages available to them. When you search a web directory you are not searching the whole web page, simply the title and key words. BUBL** (www.bubl.ac.uk/link/) **is a web directory covering all academic subject areas.**
- **Gateways and portals such as the social science gateway at Intute** (www.intute.ac.uk). **Gateways are collections of links in a particular subject area. A subject specialist will select the most appropriate resources and give a brief description of each. A portal is similar to a gateway with the addition of being personalised. You can set it to find materials that are specific to you and which it will continually update. You are much more likely to find what you want through a gateway or portal and what is there has been evaluated by someone who understands the subject area.**

All three of these offer you the facility to search, although you should remember that in both web directories and gateways you are searching key words and titles rather than the web pages themselves. Because they work in different ways, it is often worth searching on more than one search engine or directory. There are some tips for searching that apply whether you are using a search engine, a web directory or a gateway.

- **Be as precise as you can in your choice of words. Because I thought I played it, I wanted to find where the oldest Methodist pipe organ in Britain is. Just typing in 'old organ' found me all sorts of things about transplants, which was not quite what I had in mind. 'Old pipe organ' achieved a much more useful result.**
- **Try other words. If 'piano' does not find it, try 'keyboard'.**
- **Spell the word you are looking for correctly, although some search engines will offer you alternative spellings.**
- **Put the most important words first. Changing the order of the words to search for can produce different results.**

Most search facilities let you refine your search. You can search for a combination of words; exclude specific things; search for a complete phrase; search the whole web or just UK sites. Google – currently my favourite search engine – includes a very useful advanced search facility. It will also let you look for images. It is well worth spending a bit of time finding out how your favourite search engine works by reading its user guide, although if you are an activist learner, you will just want to get on with it.

When you see the results of a search, they will be presented to you in order. It might be the best order for you, but remember searching is not perfect, so it is worth looking further down the list. There is also the practice of websites paying to have their name put at the top of a list – so-called sponsored links. Reputable search engines and directories tell you when links are sponsored.

If you want to know everything about search engines, you could spend many happy hours exploring the SearchEngineWatch site at www.searchenginewatch.com/. Visiting this site will help you see how search engines work, which is a good step towards using them as a tool. Alternatively, you might simply choose to follow an internet tutorial such as the one for 'instructors' included in the Virtual Training Suite, at www.vts.intute.ac.uk/tutorial/instructor.

Teaching tip

Learners need time to develop search skills. Do not assume that they have the skills already. Early in a traditional course you would probably not send students to the library and tell them to find something relevant to read – you would direct them to a specific book and quite likely a specific chapter or even specific pages. It's exactly the same with internet resources – do not assume your learners can find appropriate websites for themselves. Give them addresses of specific web pages. Later on, when they are more competent, they can find things for themselves.

Teach your learners how to get the best from the internet by getting them to use one of the Virtual Training Suite tutorials at www.vts.intute.ac.uk/.These are excellent introductions to the internet that are subject based. They feature:

- **key websites for the subject;**
- **how to search the internet;**
- **how to review and evaluate websites;**
- **how to reflect and plan to work efficiently.**

The Virtual Training Suite is just one example of materials and services being made available through the internet specifically for further education.These are delivered through a number of organisations, in particular JISC, especially Regional Support Centres, BECTA, Janet (UK) and LSN. Some of the services and resources were initially provided for higher education but are now available to further education, too. In some cases it is taking a while to re-align the services to the different needs of FE students.

Teaching tip

Set up web quests for your learners. A web quest, according to the web quest site at the San Diego State University, (http://webquest.sdsu.edu/, is 'inquiry-oriented activity in which some or all of the information that learners interact with comes from resources on the internet'. For further details, see Chapter 6.

The rest of this chapter will focus on some of the services and materials specifically provided for further education, but do not forget that much of the value of the internet for learning is that it provides access to first-hand materials provided primarily for other purposes. Hair and beauty students have access to the product catalogues of suppliers; business studies students can examine company annual reports; geography students can see weather systems developing or track water flow in rivers.

Teaching and learning resources

National Learning Network materials (www.nln.ac.uk)

The National Learning Network (NLN) was a formal partnership of national organisations that supported ILT developments, including JISC, BECTA and LSDA (the forerunner of LSN). The intention of the partnership was to co-ordinate the actions of the different organisations and avoid unnecessary duplication of effort. Although the NLN itself no longer exists, one of its main products, the NLN materials, is a very valuable resource.

The NLN materials are small chunks of online learning specifically designed for the FE curriculum. They range from hairdressing to horticulture, ESOL to family learning and business studies to basic skills and biology. The materials were published in four phases between 2002 and 2006. They have also been made available to Adult and Community Learning and are in the process of being made available to Work Based Learning. The materials are free.

The materials are commercially produced with a variety of multimedia components. They are interactive and designed to get learners doing things. Each one contains:

- **some new learning – usually one or two learning objectives for 30 minutes or so of learning;**
- **a chance to practise the new ideas;**
- **some form of assessment.**

The materials are well worth exploring in detail; do not just take the titles. For example, the floristry level 2 materials include a section on the colour wheel, which might be used successfully with students in any subject area studying the use of colour, such as art and design, hair and beauty, painting and decorating and dress-making. My former floristry colleagues have used the colour wheel successfully both with whole classes and with learners working independently. The materials are delivered through a virtual learning environment which means that the tutor can track which learner has done what. What the tutors particularly like is that:

- **the materials give learners things to do, not just read;**
- **learners can repeat the work as often as they like;**
- **learners can work at the pace they like.**

Various support materials such as session plans and case studies in the use of the materials are also available through the NLN website. The website also contains an online guide to help tutors make the best use of the NLN materials.

Excellence Gateway (http://excellence.qia.org.uk)

Although the NLN no longer formally exists, there is a realisation that the different organisations involved – and their successors – need to work together. One manifestation of this is the Excellence Gateway. Run by the Quality Improvement Agency, it is a portal which endeavours to provide a 'complete online service for post-16 learning and skills providers … Here you will find examples of good practice from your peers, networks to support self-improvement, suppliers of improvement services plus tools and materials to support teaching and learning. Join our community and share your ideas'.

It is a good way to access a number of formerly separate websites that are well worth visiting, including ferl, ACLearn, Learning and Skills Web and Excalibur. Its coverage is much wider than simply materials – it also includes management, technology and pedagogy. One aspect to keep an eye on is the good practice database which is planned to grow significantly. Incidentally, although it calls itself a gateway, it is actually a portal because you can personalise it so it concentrates on the aspects you particularly want.

Further Education Resources for Learning (ferl.qia. org.uk/)

The FERL website proclaims that

> *FERL is an information service for all staff working within the Post Compulsory Education sector. It aims to support individuals and organisations in making effective use of ILT (Information Learning Technologies). FERL does this through a web based information service, conferences, publications and other events.*

The FERL website contains lots of useful resources including:

- **ILT materials for direct use with learners;**
- **reviews and other information about published resources;**
- **materials to help you use ILT, such as session plans;**
- **examples of other people's use of ILT set out in case studies.**

Although the site contains all this and more, it is not always easy to find what you are looking for, but it is well worth persevering. Particularly helpful is the Focus on pedagogy section with its 'store cupboard' which contains downloadable resources you can use directly. You can also submit examples of your own materials to the site.

Subject gateways

The best collection of subject gateways for further education in the UK is Intute (www.intute.ac.uk/). Intute is 'a free online service providing you with access to the very best web resources'. It is funded by JISC and organised by a network of UK universities and partners. Subject specialists select and evaluate the websites and write high quality descriptions of the resources, organised in four categories: – Arts and Humanities; Health and Life Sciences; Science, Engineering and Technology; Social Sciences. Last time I looked, it had references to 118,108 resources. You can rely on what Intute tells you about the internet resources; it is well worth a good explore.

Besides the subject-focused gateways, many colleges have created collections of web links. Some of these are available, and among the most impressive is that of the Sheffield College at http://weblearn.sheffcol.ac.uk/links/, which last time I looked contained 6,106 different links, each with a short description. There are also collections organised primarily for schools that have lots of relevant links, for example Andrew Moore's outstanding site for English teachers at www.universalteacher.org.uk.

Teaching tip

There is little point in trying to produce the biggest collection of web links for your subject area since other people will have already done that and probably have evaluated the sites for you, too. Much better to produce a small list – no more than ten – of precisely relevant sites linked to specific curriculum sections. You can also create a separate area for your learners to put references to good websites they find, each with a statement as to why it is useful and a short evaluation.

JISC resources, programmes and services

JISC – the Joint Information Systems Committee – channels funding from a range of sources, including the Learning and Skills Council and the Higher Education Funding Council to lead 'the innovative use of Information and Communications Technology to support education and research'. It does this through services such as the Regional Support Centres, programmes such as the e-Learning Innovation Programme and projects, for example trying out e-portfolios and e-assessment. Unfortunately, not everything that JISC provides is available to all parts of the Learning and Skills Sector. Work-based learning and to a lesser degree Adult and Community Learning miss out. However, much of JISC's work and resources are freely available to everyone online. Amongst the most directly useful services in our context are:

JISC collections

JISC funds access to collections and resources for FE. Some of these are free; in others, learning providers also have to contribute toward the cost. For example, in this category you will find Infotrac, a brilliant collection of full-text journals and English language newspapers. To find out what is available to you, go and talk staff in your learning centre/library. The JISC makes far more resources available to you than it is possible to list here. Go to the JISC website (www.jisc.ac.uk/) and follow the Collections link to see what is currently available.

JISCmail (www.jiscmail.ac.uk/)

You are not the only person doing the sort of work that you do and interested in the sorts of things you are interested in. JISCmail is a mailing service that enables groups of people with a common interest to network together. For example, the ILT Champions in each college usually belong to the Champions mailing list and will use it to pick the brains of other Champions. I have used the Champions list to find an online literacy and numeracy diagnostic test, to ask about what sort of interactive whiteboard people recommend and to ask about copyright issues with foreign-language newspapers. Someone usually knows the answer. The Champions list is a closed list, but many lists are open to anyone to join. You can even set up your own list.

Techdis (www.techdis.ac.uk/)

Techdis aims to improve provision for disabled staff and students in higher and further education through technology. It has databases of assistive technologies, expertise, knowledge and resources and consequently has a crucial role to play in supporting you in differentiation – meeting the needs of all learners.

Technical Advisory Service for Images (TASI) (www.tasi.ac.uk/)

TASI gives advice and support on creating, capturing, storing and retrieving digital images. Your materials can be much more effective if you include graphics, but you need to have appropriate skills and knowledge. This includes being able to scan the image or capture it from a website; to adjust its size or cut out bits you do not want; to choose between different file formats; to operate within the constraints of copyright. TASI can help you do all these.

The JISC Plagiarism Advisory Service (www.jiscpas.ac.uk/)

The JISC plagiarism service not only provides the customary advice and support you expect from JISC services but also offers a plagiarism detection tool that colleges can register for. Learners submit their work, which is compared against:

- **previously submitted student work;**
- **800 million websites;**
- **essays from cheat sites.**

The tutor receives a report showing the results of the comparison.

Regional Support Centres (www.jisc.ac.uk/rsc)

There is a JISC Regional Support Centre (RSC) in each English region, in Wales, Scotland and in Northern Ireland. The RSCs provide a range of curriculum and technical services to enable learning providers in their region to exploit the potential of e-learning. It is well worth joining the mailing list for the online newsletter that most RSCs produce in order to keep in touch with many of the developments that are going on. You do not have to read the newsletter avidly, but it will bring to your attention facilities and opportunities of potential benefit.

JISC services for managers

Janet (www.ja.net/) is the network which connects the UK's education and research organisations to each other and the rest of the world through links to the global internet. In addition it provides a range of complementary services such as text messaging.

Two valuable advisory services for managers are JISC infoNet and JISC Legal. infoNet (www.jiscinfonet.ac.uk) promotes the effective strategic planning, implementation and management of ILT. Its infokits are particularly valuable. JISC Legal (www.jisclegal.ac.uk/) is an excellent source of information relating to legal aspects of the use of ICT.

E-Learning Programme (www.elearning.ac.uk/elp)

Many of the JISC projects and initiatives relating to e-learning over the last ten years have been brought together in the e-Learning Programme. It is well worth an explore to see the bigger picture of how things are developing in key areas such as e-portfolios, e-assessment, design of learning spaces and mobile learning. It is well grounded in sound pedagogy and the case studies are particularly informative.

Other services

Online information and facilities relevant to the needs of FE learners and teachers are provided by many other organisations; for example, the examination bodies such as Edexcel (www.edexcel.org.uk/), government departments such as the Department for Education and Skills (www.dfes.gov.uk/) and quangos such as the Quality and Curriculum Authority (www.qca.org.uk/).

Teaching tip
Get into the habit of bookmarking useful sites you find. Add them to your 'favorites'. If you are not sure how, look it up using the Help facility or ask a colleague.

AbilityNet (www.abilitynet.org.uk/)

AbilityNet is a charity that provides expertise on computing and disability. Sometimes this involves tracking down complex technical solutions and specific pieces of adaptive hardware. More often, simple changes can make big improvements in the ease of use of computers, for example, changing the font or screen colour. As an FE teacher you are likely to meet some specific conditions infrequently: AbilityNet is a good place to go to find out innovative solutions to particular problems.

Smartscreen (www.smartscreen.co.uk/)

Smartscreen is an example of a learning portal, in this case provided by City and Guilds, the awarding body. Its discussion group facilities are intended to support tutors and students engaged in City and Guilds courses. If you come into this category, you can set up your own groups.

Eduserv (www.eduserv.org.uk/)

Eduserv is a not-for-profit organisation that provides services to the education community. It provides two main services appropriate to the FE sector.

- **Combined Higher Education Software Team (CHEST)** www.chest.ac.uk/ **– negotiates agreements and special offers, often on a site licence basis for the purchase of software by educational institutions – not only higher education.**
- **Athens** www.athensams.net/ **– an access management system that FE institutions can use to ensure that staff and students have access to online resources. For me, for example, it means that I can access online data sources that my college pays for from any internet computer using my Athens password.**

Using internet resources with your learners – some practical issues

Once you have found a resource your learners can use, you can simply give them the address, but this misses opportunities for learning. You should also tell them what they will learn from the site and model good evaluation practice by highlighting whose site it is and thus how the information it contains is likely to be biased or authoritative.

You may have read that it is good manners ('netiquette') to refer your learners only to the home page of a website and they then have to find the relevant part of the site if they can. You can compromise by giving your learners both the address of the home page and the address of the specific page they need – and encouraging them to use the home page information as part of the evaluation of the site.

Teaching tip

The web address for a specific page (technically called the uniform resource locator or URL) is often long and complex. Give it to your learners in electronic form if you can, such as a link in a Word document so they just click on it to be taken to the page. This avoids their making a mistake typing it in.

Finding information on the internet is only part of the process. You should also ensure that your learners know the appropriate use of what they find; and how to evaluate it.

The appropriate use of what they find

If learners simply reproduce information they find on the internet, they will learn little: it reflects a shallow approach to learning. Learning is about making sense of what has been found and building it in with existing knowledge and understanding. Learners have been known simply to copy whole chunks of text from the internet and submit it as their own work. The best way to spot this is to be familiar with the learners' work. If they pro-duce writing that uses language that is not their normal way of saying things or is more grammatically accurate, be suspicious. The JISC plagiarism service is a more formal alternative. It is advisable to have a policy to deal with copying from the internet before you meet it, and to ensure that your learners know what the policy is too.

How to evaluate the information they find

Books usually go through a rigorous checking process before publication, but anyone can put anything on the internet.There is no quality control. This means that your learn-ers should be taught to always be sceptical of what they find on the internet. At the very minimum they should ask the following questions.

1. Whose site is it? Teach them to look at the domain name as some indication of where the information has come from:
   - **.ac.uk is a UK academic site;**
   - **.edu is an overseas educational institution;**
   - **.co.uk is a UK commercial organisation;**
   - **.com is a commercial organisation;**
   - **.gov is a government department;**
   - **.org is a non-commercial organisation rather than a commercial company;**
   - **the final part of the domain name gives the country of origin; e.g. .se is Swedish; .ie is Irish; .de is German.**
2. Why is the information made available? For example, is it designed to promote a particular viewpoint?
3. How reliable is the information? How does the person doing the writing know what they are saying? How up to date is it?

It is well worth encouraging your learners to visit the Internet Detective website at www.vts.intute.ac.uk/detective for an interactive tutorial that will teach them how to eval-uate material found on websites.

Copyright

Material on the internet is subject to copyright law in exactly the same way as any other form of publication. The problem is that copyright laws were generally not written with the internet in mind, so there is not the clarity you would wish for. Strictly speaking, you are copying even when you access an internet page and your browser downloads the page into its memory. Because there would be no point in the site owner putting a page on open access on the internet in the first place unless they were happy for you to see it, it is probably OK to view a page on your own monitor, but printing it out to give to your learners or incorporating parts of it into a worksheet or handout is a different matter entirely. Here you should obtain permission.

This is not quite as restrictive as it sounds. One of the parts of many websites you usu-ally ignore is the copyright section. From now on, get into the habit of reading copyright statements of sites from which you wish to use material. Often you will find that they give permission to use for non-commercial purposes such as education. If the 'terms and conditions' statement does not give you permission, you will need to ask for it. Unless a contact person is given, the easiest thing to do is to e-mail the webmaster (there must be a gender-free term for 'webmaster'). Be precise in your request – 'I wish to include the four paragraphs of text on page www ... in a work-sheet to be used with groups of A level law students at ... . Up to 30 copies per year will be produced and acknowledge-ment of the source will be given'.

There are two further complications.

- **Copyright of the material on any one web page may actually be owned by several people. The web page owner may not have the right to give you permission to use all the page.**
- **There is debate as to whether you can hyperlink to another web page with complete freedom. If you are creating hyperlinks in web pages, it is possible to hyperlink seamlessly so that the reader doesn't know they are visiting another site. This strengthens the advice set out earlier that it is good practice to link to the home page of a website.**

For further guidance on copyright issues, visit the copyright pages of the Patent Office at www.ipo.gov.ukfcopy/ or the Copyright Licensing Agency website at www.cla.co.uk/. The UK Patent Office website is intended to answer practical questions about copyright and intellectual property.

PRACTICAL TASK PRACTICAL TASK PRACTICAL TASK PRACTICAL TASK PRACTICAL TASK

You will notice that the Patent Office reference is not to the home page: however, I have made clear whose website it is I have by contrast referenced to the home page of the Copyright Licensing Agency site and left you to find the link to the relevant section. Was that easy enough? Could your learners find an equivalent internal site link?

Images are particularly tempting. It is so easy in Internet Explorer to right-click on an image and choose 'Save target as...' or 'Save picture as...' If you click on the Images tab in Google before you search, it will often produce thousands of images, some of them very appropriate to what you want.

Teaching tip
On the basis of what you have read in the above section and seen on the two copyright websites I have referred you to, make a decision to respect copyright. This will be more comfortable for your conscience and also model appropriate values for your learners. Where you use internet sources, acknowledge them.

The best resources – your colleagues and your learners

In the same way that your colleagues and your learners are your best resources in face-to-face teaching, they are also your best resource in ILT and e-learning.

Your colleagues
- **Use your colleagues as part of your reflective practice process. Talk to them about what you want to do and what happens when you try it out.**
- **Ask your colleagues how they use e-learning and the internet.**
- **Do not be afraid to ask for help if you need it. Ask your colleagues to show you how to carry out a particular e-learning function rather than asking them to do it for you.**

Your learners

- Collect electronic examples of learner work to use with subsequent groups as a standard for comparison.
- Use your learners' technical knowledge – but do not assume they are always right. They may be very experienced in playing computer games but probably have limited experience of operating computer networks.
- Use your learners' enthusiasm. Ask them to create resources and activities such as a webquest other learners can use.
- Get feedback from your learners on how effective the use of e-learning is for them. Ask what things you do work well and what things you do get in the way. Amend your practice in the light of what they say.
- Use your learners to make decisions, so you do not have to make them all. Your learners may well like the idea that you and they are trying out different ways of learning. Give them choices about the use of e-learning: do they want to produce a Power-Point presentation or write an essay, and what would they gain from each?
- Encourage learners to share what they find on the internet. Model that it is acceptable that they know more than you do about some things.

The internet is a tremendous resource for your learners and increasingly resources targeted at post-16 education are being made available. Make sure you get the best out of it.

REFLECTIVE TASK

Review the resources and services identified in this chapter. Identify two resources and two services that are potentially of value to you. Write a paragraph or two in your diary or on your blog on how they might help learning and what you have to do to introduce them.

SIGNPOST This chapter has considered the range of ILT resources and services available for your use in FE. By now you should have lots of ideas and lots of things to try out.

The next – and final – chapter considers how you can introduce e-learning into your practice, and what things are likely to get in the way.

Websites

In this chapter, the websites have been included in the text.

Visual overview

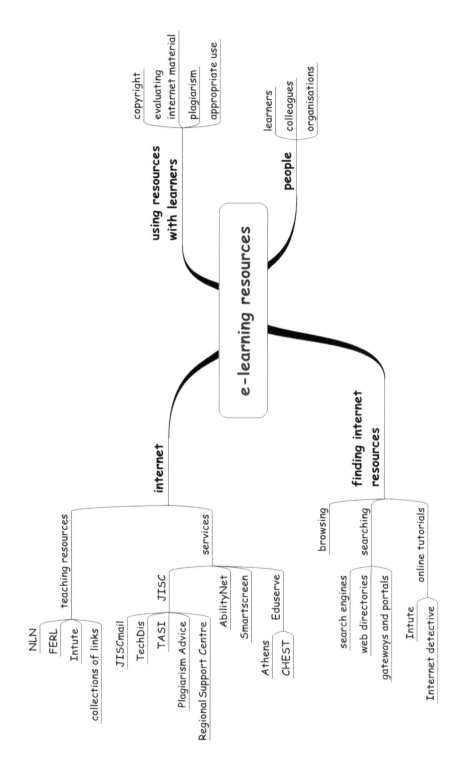

using resources with learners

- copyright
- evaluating internet material
- plagiarism
- appropriate use

people

- learners
- colleagues
- organisations

e-learning resources

internet

teaching resources
- NLN
- FERL
- Intute
- collections of links

services
- JISCmail
- TechDis
- TASI
- JISC
- Plagiarism Advice
- Regional Support Centre
- AbilityNet
- Smartscreen
- Athens
- CHEST
- Eduserve

finding internet resources

- browsing
- searching
  - search engines
  - web directories
  - gateways and portals
- online tutorials
  - Intute
  - Internet detective

9
Introducing e-learning

This chapter will help you to:

- **identify barriers to introducing e-learning and some strategies for overcoming them;**
- **evaluate reasons for not using e-learning;**
- **adopt strategies to develop systematically your own use of e-learning;**
- **consider the introduction of ILT and e-learning on an institutional basis.**

LLUK Standards relevant to this chapter include:
BP3.1, BP5.1, CP3.5, DP1.2, EP1.2.

Reactions to ILT

I have spent nearly 20 years trying to foster the use of ILT: there is still a way to go. The government has invested considerable amounts of money in the use of e-learning and set up all sorts of support structures: a minority of lecturers use e-learning as a major part of their toolkit. The introduction of ILT in further education makes an excellent case study of how change happens, but not always as planned. It exemplifies how people respond to change, the barriers to change and how change can be managed. Somebody will write a doctoral thesis on this soon, or maybe has already. Understanding change in general can help you through the process of introducing ILT into your own teaching.

I have encountered widely differing reactions from my colleagues in response to e-learning initiatives. I would broadly divide the reactions into three categories:

- **resisters, who cannot envisage using e-learning in spite of everything done to encourage them;**
- **enthusiasts, who will use e-learning regardless;**
- **pragmatists, who will use e-learning if they can see achievable benefits for themselves and/or their learners. This is the biggest category.**

These three categories conceal a spectrum of reactions, which are set out in Figure 9.1.

The reactions range from the absolute rejection ('Over my dead body') to excited enthusiasm ('The best thing since sliced bread'), with many variations in between. In Figure 9.1, I visualise a progression clockwise starting at one o'clock, although you might choose to change the order of the elements.

Resisters simply refuse to consider e-learning as a realistic possibility. This may be how they respond to any change in life in general, because they have a fear of the unknown or because they feel threatened, for example by a conviction that e-learning will lead eventually to redundancy. Enthusiasts seize upon the discovery of e-learning and use it for everything. In doing so they are actively exploring new territory, which can be an

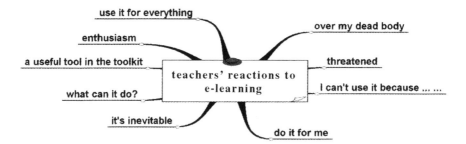

Figure 9.1 Reactions to e-learning

exciting experience. However, the danger is that enthusism for the technology clouds judgement. Just because you can use e-learning for something does not necessarily mean that you should do it. Things that worked well before the introduction of e-learning may be forgotten and replaced by less effective practice. Death by PowerPoint replaces the sparing use of appropriate overhead transparencies.

Most teachers adopt a pragmatic response. Teacher training courses are based on a model of continuous improvement through reflective practice. Reflective practice, based on the work of Schön (1983), is the concept that, throughout your teaching career, you endeavour to teach better and improve your learners' learning by reviewing what happens in your teaching. There is often no absolute right or wrong in teaching. Teachers are professionals rather than technicians because we face a unique situation – and hence unique decisions – every time we work with students. Reflection is vital to maintaining the effectiveness of that process.

In the context of reflective practice, the pragmatist wants to find out what e-learning can do and to add it as a tool to the teaching toolkit alongside other effective tools. Thus to the pragmatist, adopting e-learning is about increasing the number of options available. For example, conducting a learning-needs questionnaire manually takes much time and effort, so much so that it might not be carried out. The same questionnaire conducted online takes a matter of minutes and provides useful information for differentiating between learners. Most teachers would welcome that. Not all pragmatists adopt a positive attitude. Some expect everything to be done for them and become passive. Others reluctantly accept that e-learning is inevitable because it reflects the way that society is evolving. They will use it, not because they are convinced by its effectiveness but because they are required to use it. They have no choice.

Enthusiasts, pragmatists and resisters all face barriers that hinder the adoption of e-learning and which have to be overcome. Resisters are of course absolutely certain that the barriers are insurmountable; enthusiasts are prone to dismiss the barriers. Pragmatists just want a solution that works. They carry out a sort of cost-benefit analysis – determining the benefits resulting from the change compared with the costs of achieving it.

PRACTICAL TASK PRACTICAL TASK PRACTICAL TASK PRACTICAL TASK PRACTICAL TASK

- On the basis of the descriptions I have given, decide whether you are a resister, an enthusiast or a pragmatist. What do you think are the consequences of your viewpoint?
- List barriers that have limited your own use of e-learning.
- Compare your list with the reasons my colleagues have given me, as set out in Table 9.1.

For a while I have been collecting reasons that teachers give for not adopting e-learning. How many of these do you empathise with? Put a tick in the right-hand column of Table 9.1 if you can hear yourself saying it.

Perceived barrier	Is this you?
My students will know more than me.	
I don't know what to do if it goes wrong.	
I do not have the skills.	
I do not have the time.	
I haven't got a computer at home.	
I can't get easy access to a computer at work.	
My computer is too old/keeps breaking down.	
I don't want to change.	
I'm alright as I am.	
Nobody else is doing it.	
Students will think that they need not come to classes any more – they can do it on their own.	
I do not want my students to work on their own with a computer all the time.	
I've got innovation overload.	
I've always done it like this.	
It's the thin end of the wedge.	
I'm too near retirement.	
I'm only part-time.	
My students cannot afford computers.	

Table 9.1 Reasons for not adopting e-learning

Many teachers teach using the methods that they experienced as students. In other words, if, you learned history successfully when your teacher lectured at you, you will tend to use the lecture to teach history. Since, with some exceptions, e-learning is relatively new across the curriculum, few teachers will have learned their subjects through e-learning. This means that, for teachers to use e-learning, they must move away from their own experience as learners.

Disadvantages of introducing e-learning

In Chapter 2 we explored the benefits of e-learning. There has to be another side of the equation. What are the disadvantages of adopting e-learning?

Opportunity cost

To an economist, the real cost of e-learning within further education is not the £74 million invested between 1999 and 2002 by the government and the further £300 million found by colleges. That is mere money. Economists are concerned with the use of resources and a more realistic measure is opportunity cost – what you have to give up in order to use resources in a particular way. The opportunity costs of ILT include the following.

- **The resources and materials that could have been bought with the same money: furniture, staff time, books, equipment – except of course, if it were not for the focus on ILT, that money would not have been available.**
- **The use of time. Would using the staff and learner time in different ways have produced a greater impact on learning?**

Loss of perspective

In the introduction of e-learning, colleges often pass through a period of emphasis on the technology before they focus on the curriculum. This shows itself in many ways, such as heated discussion about the specification of computers or network software rather than learning needs and how can ICT help to meet them. The conse-quence is that equipment and software are acquired which are then under-used. I know of a college with a video-conferencing system that is used at most once a year. It was acquired because a senior manager thought it would be a good facility to have, but no one asked the shop-floor teachers. Organisations need to mature in their use of ICT to the point where they see it as a means to an end rather than an end in itself. In other words, they think e-learning rather than IT.

Meeting different learner needs

As we become more aware of differentiation, we must accept that some learners do not find using a computer an effective way of learning. We tend to assume that, because sig-nificant sectors of society use ICT, all learners, especially young learners, benefit from using it.

It must be used well

There are particular dangers with e-learning if it is not used well. Learners might become more isolated, spending extended periods of time working alone at the computer. Extensive use of the internet encourages a knowledge acquisition model of learning.

We need to understand changes in working practices and funding of courses

ILT opens up different ways of working that we have to adapt to. In addition to under-standing the pedagogy involved, tutoring a fully online course raises management issues about funding and working practice.

- **How much tutoring time will the award take? How much tutor support will the course members need?**
- **Can you tutor the course from home? Do your managers trust you enough to do this? If they do, will they contribute towards internet costs? What would the effect of working from home be on the effectiveness of your relationships with colleagues at work? What would the college gain or lose from tutors working at home?**

- Further education funding is primarily linked to learner attendance at classes where a register is kept. Although there is special provision for distance learning courses, there is not yet a funding mechanism that accurately reflects e-learning, especially in a blended learning context.

The introduction of e-learning on an individual basis

It is helpful to think of the introduction of e-learning into your own teaching as a project. This means that you plan and implement it in a systematic way. You look for possible pitfalls and decide how to tackle them. Lockett (2007) suggests that the person managing an ILT project needs four qualities. In the context of the individual teacher introducing e-learning, that person is you. You need to have:

- energy **to provide the momentum to start the project in the first place and to keep it going through to completion – you need perseverance and enthusiasm;**
- ability **to know about the new technology and, more importantly, understanding of the teaching and learning process;**
- vision **to be able to project your ideas into the future, to have an idea about what successful completion of the project will look like – that is not to say that what finally emerges from a project is what you expected when you started;**
- motivation **few further education teachers are in the profession for the money, but the motivation we generally respond to is the benefit for both colleagues and learners.**

There is a very useful infokit on the infoNet website telling you all you need to know about managing a project, whether it is a big project or a small one (www.jiscinfonet.ac.uk/InfoKits/project-management). Alternatively, Bill Lockitt (2007) has written a very helpful, relevant guide.

A project has three stages:

1. planning the project;
2. implementing the project;
3. reviewing the impact of the project.

Adopting a project approach is sensible because it encourages you to develop your use of ILT in a structured and thoughtful way. In planning the project you should establish clearly the project's scope, objectives and outcomes and break the work down into manageable, achievable tasks. In implementing the project, you should negotiate appropriate support. In reviewing the impact of the project, you should measure the extent to which the project's objectives have been achieved.

You probably would expect to do all of these, but there are also things that you might not initially think of, but which should be incorporated in good practice. In the planning stage you not only have to identify who will benefit from the project, but also achieve a balance between what you gain and what other stakeholders gain. The need to involve other people is significant in every stage – in planning, implementing and reviewing. Many projects have failed because only the originator has any ownership of the work. With a small innovation you may choose not to adopt a full project approach, but it is still worth thinking through the issues the project approach raises.

A project approach has other benefits. It makes the innovation more manageable by providing boundaries and a timescale that has an end point. There comes a point where you have to make a decision about whether to incorporate the development into your routine teaching. In addition, it gives permission to learn from the elements of your innovation that are not successful. When you try out a new idea that is not successful, do not think of it as being a waste of time. You will benefit from the experience and if your manager is wise, she or he will support your effort. All change involves risk taking (although not as much risk as changing nothing). What is essential is that you learn from the experience.

You also need support. This support might be provided by the following sources.

- **Your organisation might deliver it through a formal structure such as ILT Champions. Find out what is on offer to you. Staff development processes might offer you time or a mentoring service to support you extending your skills.**
- **You may have a mentor relationship with a colleague.**
- **A positive manager will encourage you to reflect on your teaching and support your endeavours to improve it.**

Change always involves risk: you are changing away from the predictable. It is quite possible that change may not work, especially in the short run, although it is more likely to work if it is well thought through. 'If you always do what you've always done, you'll always get what you've always got'. What the reflective practitioner wants is improvement. There is increasing recognition that to move forward often involves a risk of failure and if you have shared the process with your manager, it is more likely that the process will be a beneficial one for both of you. Look for the support that is available and use it.

Teaching tip

The best support can come from your learners. When you introduce new e-learning into your teaching, involve your learners. Tell them what you are doing and why. Ask them for evidence about the change from their perspective and suggestions for improvement. This is all part of the process of giving learners ownership of their own learning. Making your learners aware of the learning process is part of teaching them how to learn. That is far more valuable than teaching facts.

It never fails to amuse and at times frustrate me that we often fail to put the principles of teaching and learning into practice in the way we run our colleges. Research shows that grading assignments can be harmful because a high mark makes a learner complacent and a low mark discourages; yet inspection processes often grade observed lessons. We teach communication as a key skill, yet we are not good at listening to each other. We stress the importance of positive constructive feedback (the 'medal and mission' described by Petty, 2004) yet are not good at giving it to our colleagues. Don't forget, that just as you would respond to positive constructive feedback from a colleague, so it is part of the role of being a colleague for you to do the same.

The introduction of ILT on an organisational basis

Managing change on an institutional basis is itself the object of detailed study. The widespread introduction of ILT certainly necessitates significant change in organisations. The change itself has at least four different dimensions. Table 9.2 identifies the dimensions, sets out what each might involve in the large-scale introduction of ILT into an institution and gives an example of the sort of issue that might arise.

Issue	Example	Potential problems
technical	• installation of hardware and software • training staff in the use of the kit and the software	• cost of innovation
strategic	• clarification of the role of the ILT innovation in the achievement of key objectives of the organisation such as developing workplace training or lifelong learning	• the innovation becomes an end in itself rather than a means to enable the organisation to achieve its strategic objectives
political	• achieving support from stakeholders • achieving consent from those who may be threatened by the change	• managers who feel their status is threatened by the change may work to oppose it • staff may feel they have no ownership of the innovation
structural	• organising management responsibilities to produce clear responsibilities	• restructuring takes time for people to adapt to new roles

Table 9.2 Dimensions of change

Johnson and Scholes (1997) consider styles of managing change. They describe a continuum of approaches, as set out in Figure 9.2.

coercion	direction	intervention	participation	education
manager imposes all aspects of change	manager sets the direction of change and how it will be done	manager retains overall control but delegates aspects	manager delegates change to small group or taskforce	full communication to everyone involved

Figure 9.2 Styles of managing strategic change

At one extreme of the continuum is coercion, where change is imposed. This is rarely successful as a strategy, except in emergencies. At the other extreme is education, where change involves lots of discussion, often in small group meetings and takes a long time. This may be equally ineffective because there can be a lack of clarity as to the purpose of the innovation. In between are styles where there is more or less authoritarian direction, more or less discussion and more or less delegation and ownership for all those involved in the innovation. Crucial to these styles is the communication system chosen and how effective it is. The more complex the changes that are to be initiated, the richer the communication that needs to take place. It needs to be interactive (how much communication in the management process is one-way?) and relevant to each individual.

Within a learning provider, management of the large-scale introduction of ILT may adopt any of these styles – and, within that, different managers may adopt different approaches. Communication may be more or less effective.

PRACTICAL TASK PRACTICAL TASK PRACTICAL TASK PRACTICAL TASK PRACTICAL TASK

Imagine that the organisation you work for wants to implement a large-scale ILT innovation such as the provision of a computer and interactive whiteboard in every room. As a member of the teaching staff, consider how this should be carried out. In particular think about:

- how you should be told of the plan in the first place;
- how you could contribute your ideas;
- what support would need to be provided for you to exploit the new facility;
- what reactions you or your colleagues might have;
- what your managers could do to build on positive ideas and break down resistance.

Action research

An alternative approach to innovation is action research. Action research is a structured cycle of systematic action and reflection, which has as its focus the improvement of your practice as a teacher. It provides an appropriate structure for the introduction of any change into your teaching. Action research follows a cycle, set out in Figure 9.3.

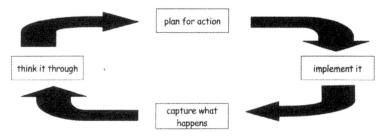

Figure 9.3 The action research cycle

The cycle works like this.

1. You decide you want to change something in your teaching – in this case, to introduce an aspect of e-learning. You plan to implement the change.
2. You implement the change.
3. You identify the results of the change and record what happens.
4. You try to make sense of the outcomes, to understand what happens.
5. You compare where you are with where you wanted to be and, if necessary, plan for future action and repeat the cycle.

Action research is a respectable approach to formal academic research, in particular because it deals with the issue of how you can carry out valid research when you are personally involved in a situation. When adopting an action research approach to introducing an aspect of e-learning into your teaching, you do not have to carry it out to the rigorous standards required by published research and you can go for the quick and dirty. However, it is worthwhile considering some of the practices you would have to adopt if it were research for publication.

- **Decide in advance how you would recognise success. Write it down.**
- **Collect the results of the change systematically.**

- Look for valid evidence. For example, you could interview learners or ask a colleague to observe class sessions rather than relying on your own impressions.
- Where possible, find evidence that comes from different perspectives so that one can act as a check on the other (this process is called triangulation).
- Explore relevant ideas from reading to help you understand what is happening.

An action research approach will give you a structure within which to implement your development, and let you focus on whether your innovation has a positive effect on learner experience. To learn more about action research, McNiff's (1988) book is a readable introduction.

REFLECTIVE TASK

Now you have reached the end of this book, make a personal pledge to explore e-learning. If you do not currently exploit much of the potential of e-learning in your teaching; decide on one small action you could take that would extend your use of e-learning. If you do currently use e-learning decide on one new-to-you aspect of e-learning to exploit next. In both cases, write down three tasks you would have to carry out in order to do it. Put them in a logical order. Do the top one!.

I have a collection of trite sayings that I fondly imagine are helpful but I suspect may simply irritate. I do not claim that they are original. They include such phrases as 'when all else fails, read the instructions' and 'measure twice, cut once'. The relevant saying here is 'To finish a journey you have to start it'. To develop your use of e-learning you have to begin somewhere.

At the end of each of the previous chapters the signpost has pointed forward to the content of the following chapter. This is the last chapter: what follows this? Essentially, what teacher training courses call 'the long teaching practice' – in other words, the rest of your teaching life. So what is the strategy for successfully introducing e-learning into your teaching? This book has promoted a perspective that e-learning should be part of the toolkit of every teacher, to be selected when appropriate and complementing the other tools in the kit. But this tool is different: in particular it has the potential for real differentiation, for learning to meet the needs of each individual learner. So how do you do it? In the same way that you would eat an elephant. One mouthful at a time.

REFERENCES AND FURTHER READING REFERENCES AND FURTHER READING

Johnson, G. and Scholes, K. (1997) *Exploring corporate strategy* (fourth edition). London: Prentice Hall.

Lockett, B. (2007) *Putting the Q into quality project management.* London: Learning and Skills Network.

McNiff1, J. (1988) *Action research: principles and practice*. London: Routledge.

Petty, G. (2004) *Teaching today* (third edition). Cheltenham: Stanley Thornes.

Schön, D. A. (1983) *The reflective practitioner: how professionals think in action*. New York: Basic Books.

Websites
www.jiscinformat.ac.uk/ infokits

Visual overview

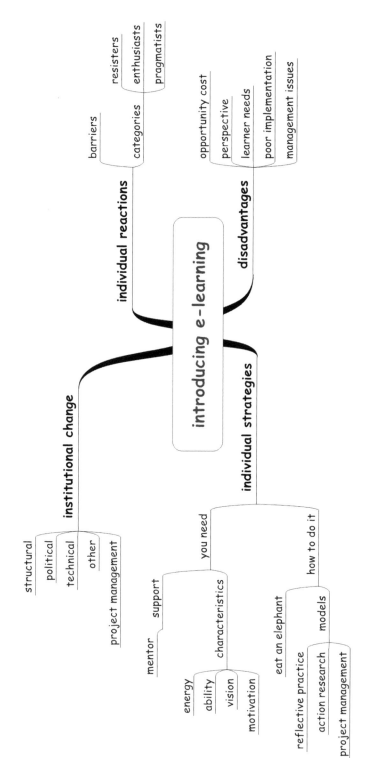

Glossary of acronyms

BECTA	British Educational Communications and Technology Agency	The government's lead organisation for supporting the strategic use of technology in learning	www.becta.org.uk
CHEST	Combined Higher Education Software Team	Negotiates agreements and offers for use by the educational community	www.chest.ac.uk
CLAIT	Computer Literacy and Information Technology	Foundation computer skills qualification	www.ocr.org.uk/
ECDL	European Computer Driving Licence	Broad coverage computer skills qualification	www.ecdl.co.uk/
FERL	Further Education Resources for Learning	Information service supporting effective use of ILT. So many resources it is not always easy to find what you want – but well worth it	ferl.qia.org.uk/
ICT	information and communication technology	IT kit linked together for communication and networking	
ILT	information and learning technology	ICT used for the purpose of education – both direct learning and the wider business	
IT	information technology	The kit – computer, mobile phone, camcorder	
JANET (UK)	Joint Academic Network	service linking FE and HE institutions to the internet	www.ja.net/
JISC	Joint Information Services Committee	Provides guidance, advice and services to the FE/HE education sectors. Channel for funding	www.jisc.ac.uk/
LLUK	Lifelong Learning UK	The Sector Skills Council for post-16 education and training. Devised the standards for teacher training awards	
LSC	Learning and Skills Council	Main funding source for post-16 education and training	www.lsc.gov.uk/
LSN	Learning and Skills Network	Delivers quality improvement and staff development programmes, research and consultancy	

LSDA	Learning and Skills Development Agency	Development organisation now split into QIA and LSN. Still continues in Northern Ireland	
NILTA	National Information and Learning Technologies Association	Membership organisation aiming to encourage staff to be actively involved with ILT. Part of the Association of Colleges	www.axnilta.co.uk/
NLN	National Learning Network	Overall name for partner organisations leading government ILT initiatives. Website good starting point	www.nln.ac.uk/
QIA	Quality Improvement Agency	Commissioning agency for quality improvement in the learning and skills sector	
RDN	Resource Discovery Network	Old name for Intute. Gathers, indexes, describes and evaluates resources. Well worth an explore. Virtual Training Suite is excellent	www.intute.ac.uk/
RSC	Regional Support Centre	Supports all ILT developments in learning providers in each region. Find yours!	www.jisc.ac.uk
TASI	Technical Advisory Services for Images	Advice on everything to do with images	www.tasi.ac.uk/

Index